OUT OF THE ASHES

A Handbook for Starting Over

**Patrick J. McDonald
and
Claudette M. McDonald**

**Paulist Press
New York/Mahwah, N.J.**

Cover design by Cynthia Dunne

Library of Congress Cataloging-in-Publication Data

McDonald, Patrick J., 1939–
    Out of the ashes : a handbook for starting over / Patrick J. McDonald and Claudette M. McDonald
     p. cm.
    Includes bibliographical references.
    ISBN 0-8091-3695-3 (alk. paper)
    1. Life change events—Religious aspects—Christianity. 2. Loss (Psychology)—Religious aspects—Christianity. 3. Adjustment (Psychology)—Religious aspects—Christianity. 4. Peace of mind—Religious aspects—Christianity. 5. Consolation. I. McDonald, Claudette M., 1948– . II. Title
BV4908.5.M355 1997
248.8′6—dc20   96-44805
                                                       CIP

Published by Paulist Press
997 Macarthur Boulevard
Mahwah, NJ 07430

Printed and bound in the
United States of America

CONTENTS

We are especially grateful to our advisor and editor,
Mr. Doug Fisher. His support, guidance, and honest criticism
have enabled us to continue to write.

Introduction

We believe wisdom begins with listening: listening to an inner voice, listening to the voices of others, listening for the voice of the sacred. We place the term *listening* within its widest possible context: to hear with the ears as well as the heart, to see, to absorb, to sense, to explore intuitively the churnings of life in a way that opens up a rich new perspective. Indeed, listening offers the context for bringing new dreams to life.

Our reflections begin the same morning that the nation awakens to the news of a major tragedy. We turn to watch a continuous stream of live television images, captured in the shadows of the twisted carcass of the bombed-out federal building in Oklahoma City.

We stare in silence as a small army of rescue workers feverishly dig to open the building to steal back whatever life tenaciously survives under the mess of twisted metal and collapsed concrete. We rejoice as the shell of a building grudgingly yields the living here and there, like the slow payback of a mean-spirited slot machine.

We hear a chorus of mothers pleading with God for the safety of their children, still trapped under the collapsed floor of the day care center. Reverence for the suffering families forces us to drop our writing task for the day and simply pray for them.

Rumors drift like dirty smoke over the heartland,

searching for substance before settling into serious talk of a terrorist connection with the Middle East. They finally solidify into hard news that the obscene specter of violence lies closer to our shores than Americans first wanted to believe.

We return to our writing in probing, half-focused efforts, as days gray into nights of losing hope that larger numbers of the living might be snatched from the realm of the dead. As reality slowly reconstructs for the victims and their families, we finally get an opportunity to stand back from the madness and gather a perspective.

At first assessment, two images stand out in dark relief from the thousands of impressions captured on videotape. First, the bombed-out hulk of the federal building is now a leering icon for the absurdity of life in our time. America has changed. Big government, stout buildings, and elaborate security measures no longer guarantee anyone's safety.

Second, there are the visible efforts of victims and families to make sense out of what happened to them. We hear great mourning and witness a potpourri of funeral rituals. Each rite affirms a resting place for those who died and a tempered life for those who remain.

We now turn our conversation toward the rightful place of mythology in life, noting an almost instinctual capacity of the human species to make sense out of the senseless. Like countless others who lived and died before our brief time in history, modern pilgrims look for signs of new life when confronted with the collapse of the old.

The Egyptians saw a rebirth of energy in the symbol of the phoenix bird. Attired in glorious plumage, the phoenix follows the track of the sun upon rising from the ashes of its own funeral pyre. Ancient celebrations of the changing seasons include a homage to the constancy of life within the continued cycle of death, decay, and regeneration.

Native Americans send their prayers aloft on the wings of an eagle. Jesus tells the story of the seed that falls into the ground and dies in order to live. The Buddhists speak of building our lives on the firm foundation of nothingness.

Change, growth, and life transitions are all around us. Not every change is dramatic, painful, or complicated, for many people welcome them into their lives and delight in their evolution. This book, however, describes the process of change at a deeper level. Our selection of real examples and use of strong metaphors describe changes that are serious and often cataclysmic. They bring with them powerful feelings of loss, serious re-examination of values, and hard efforts to rebuild. These changes are usually unwelcome, leaving their victims feeling vulnerable and helpless. It is in this state that the hard questions about life, death, love, human destiny, and the importance of a spirituality naturally evolve.

"What happened to my beliefs, my reality?" people ask. "Where do I start? How do I get underway? Where do I find the wisdom and energy I need to start all over again? Can I trust myself? Can I trust others? Can I trust the stars? Can I trust God?"

To respond to these questions, we will suggest some ways to listen to the wisdom hidden within your person. We will also suggest some ways to listen to the voices of others, and uncover the hidden caches of wisdom within them.

We will invite you to drink from the sources, examine some of their assumptions, then incorporate these explorations into a redefined sense of self. We will encourage you to trust your intuition as the foundation for a maturing spirituality. We will share with you a model of process, and hope that the model will sustain you as you confront new transitions during other chapters of your life. In this way, your new dreams will be based upon a more stable foundation. Finally, we invite you to use the book as a handbook, allowing it to guide you through current and future changes.

We turn again to watch the images of rebuilding presented to us by the television screen. We listen to talk of "moving on." The phoenix bird begins to stir, shaking the ashes from its spreading plumage as it prepares for flight. Life begins to take form again.

Explore with us some new possibilities for life and love that evolve out of real losses, and in doing so, awaken to the wisdom that sleeps within.

1.

SOARING

The Human Spirit

There is a majestic quality to the human spirit, especially when it soars aloft under the most trying conditions.

As the punishing winter of 1996 began to deepen, our local newspaper reported a nineteen-year-old Native American dead from electrocution, sustained when he climbed to the top of a power pole. The media first speculated that his death might be a freak accident, but the story came to life as police investigated the incident more thoroughly.

The young man was an employee of a local tower company, working there since high school. Each day, he climbed as high as 1,000 feet above ground level to maintain radio, television, and special communication towers in Nebraska, Iowa, and Illinois.

The late afternoon of the accident, he ascended the power pole in an effort to free a red-tailed hawk, trapped in the tangle of wires and transmission hardware. He nearly succeeded in freeing the bird, but the frightened animal spread its wings, contacted the transmission lines, and the electrical current passed through both of them. They died instantly.

The young man was a Yaqui Indian by birth. Born on

an Arizona reservation, he lived with his family for a time in California, then moved with them to the Midwest when life on the West Coast became too violent.

Both his mother and father expressed astonishment that so many of his local friends came for the funeral. Those who gathered shared their stories, remembered him fondly, then spoke in awe about his tireless love for the environment, especially for the great birds of prey. The red-tailed hawk that led to his death became an important symbol of life at his funeral. His family laid it to rest in the same casket as its rescuer, its wing and tail feathers spread wide across the dead man's breast.

In his family's possession rests a letter from the U.S. Department of the Interior, which reads, "In compliance with policy…this letter is authorization to possess one red-tailed hawk found electrocuted in Des Moines on December 5, 1995. The hawk is to be used for official Native American burial ceremonies for your son." At the end of the service, his family awarded him a new name: *White Eagle*.

As telling as this story is about the capacity of the human spirit to mimic the flight of the great birds of prey, most stories of the spirit gain poignancy in their telling within the context of the human struggle for survival.

The stories invite us to address the hard questions of life: what makes life worth living, and what is worth dying for? What infuses life with meaning and substance? Where do I look to find the deeper values in life? What excites me, and what deadens my spirit? Where do I discover lasting wisdom?

We have discovered in our work with people over the last twenty-five years, that these deep questions about the significance of life burst into consciousness at a time when change and loss are most real.

⊩ The Reality of Change ⊩

Change can steal into a person's life as silently as the onset of a malignant growth. Like an alien creature, once attached, it slowly robs the person of energy, spirit, then life. Change can also impact as calamitously as a bomb blast, making no discrimination about its victims, caring nothing about its damage. Whether its onset is subtle or calamitous, change can be traumatic and devastating, altering the course of life in less than a second.

Even though the forms of change vary immensely, their sources can generally be identified, offering the victims a clear focus for their emptiness, disillusionment, and anger. We find another kind of change that seems almost epidemic in our society, but the roots of the change remain hidden. They lie somewhere within the web of a complex organizational structure, shifting business environment, or an overly specialized network of agencies and departments. Change within these contexts can be especially maddening. An example will shed some light on what we observe.

"I could tell there was something wrong the moment he stepped out of the Lexus," said the thirty-five year old executive wife.

"I have learned to watch for signs: facial expressions, how he carries himself, his hesitancy in pulling on up the driveway. This time, his face gave him away. His jaw was set. No smile. He didn't even respond to the kids when they ran out to greet him. He walked by me, but made no eye contact.

"We finally got a chance to talk, late in the evening

when the kids were tucked in," she continued, pausing now and then to refocus. "I almost died before he told me...what happened. He told me someone sent a fax that morning from the home office in New York, announcing that the projected buyout of the company was complete. The company is now a subsidiary of Micronet, and all district managers are replaced by Micronet personnel under the reorganization agreement."

She became animated as the complexity of her story grew, elevating her hands toward the early evening sky in a gesture of helplessness. The atmosphere seemed inappropriately tense for a Sunday evening cookout.

"A *fax*," she repeated. Her listeners tensed. "A *fax*! After working so hard for that organization. When I think about all the moves, all the sacrifices we made, all that we have done to live up to the image of the happy corporate family— and he gets a *fax* announcing his job is being terminated!"

Her husband nodded, shrugged his shoulders, then looked blankly at the placid surface of the swimming pool.

"He can't even get at the source of all these changes to gain a fair hearing," she continued. "The *fax* came from some new name out of the New York office. The entire upper management group set themselves up royally during the secret negotiations, bailing out of the place in their golden parachutes. They got everything they wanted and we got nothing. Talk about feeling betrayed."

Her listeners looked stunned. There was quiet for a time. "So what are you going to do, Jane?" pleaded a soft voice.

"Right now we just don't know what we're going to do. Jim is just that age where the job market closes down. They're hiring much younger people now, two or three of them for what Jim was making, and these kids are happy to have it. His MBA makes him overqualified. So right now, I just don't know what we're going to do: move on, perhaps—look for other work—keep hoping that something opens up. We just don't know." No one spoke.

"We will get enough severance pay to survive for six months," she went on. "We'll have to survive one way or another." Her voice wavered slightly. "But don't let me throw a damper on the party. Let's have a good time. We'll survive."

The silence was filled with the rhythmic chatter of evening insects and the laughter of children in the side yard.

Stories like this abound in the current American experience, and they unfold at precisely the wrong time. Those caught up in the complexity of change find it almost impossible to identify the sources, and this can be maddening. Disappointment, hurt, anger, and a gaggle of other emotions hunger for a focus. A thousand questions about the causes, the sources, the realities of change, remain undirected and unanswered. Typical responses to the perceived injustice are either strained silence or anxious chatter that remains unheard.

‖ The Five Processes of Change ‖

All stories of change begin somewhere and end somewhere. In the silent gap between the beginning and the end, we find an endless stream of stories, as people sift and search for ways to chart a new direction. In the process, however, they become different people, moving toward a deeper knowledge of life, love, change, and growth. As they live and struggle, they usually achieve what we call engendered wisdom.

Through our own sifting of their stories, we identify a series of processes that remain consistent in every account. These processes mark not only the beginning, middle and end of their personal drama, they chart the evolution of genuine change from its beginning state of emptiness, to an embrace of hard-won wisdom. We also suggest that these same processes are the building blocks of a mature spirituality. We will briefly explore them below, then expand on them as specific chapters in this book.

‖ Process 1: Disintegration ‖

Like the stories in the examples above, the reality of change descends in an unwanted form. It forces a person, family, or extended network of friends to face the dramatic proposition that life will never be the same.

Not only does the structure of life change dramatically, so do many of the underlying beliefs that have focused, formed, and directed life itself. The surface of reality is usually strewn with the wreckage of assumptions that no longer work: "If you work hard, you'll get ahead." "Loyalty to another person will be rewarded with loyalty in return." "If you love someone enough, they will change."

In brief, life collapses into a demoralized state of confusion and emptiness. The reservoir of wisdom runs dry. Energy degenerates. Dreams die. Questions about survival abound. Listlessness and discouragement govern each day. Some modern writers refer to this state of ennui as the loss of soul.

‖ Process 2: Sifting ‖

We liken this process to the Oklahoma City rescue workers' tasks: systematically sifting through the ruins of the federal building, looking for any sign of life to animate their continued efforts.

The initial task for the individual confronting change is to sift through a collection of beliefs, values, goals, attitudes, myths, and dreams, then examine which of them are dead and which remain alive.

"What happened?" people ask. "Why did my dreams die? What is left for me now? What did I buy into about this company taking care of me? Why doesn't love work? Who wants me at this age? Where do I go from here? What do I carry away with me, and what do I leave behind?"

The process of sifting can bring with it an encounter with enlightened self-discovery. It can also bring an agonizing realization that some fantasies have died forever.

In sifting, the person learns to listen for the voice of wisdom. It can speak from the unexplored strata of personal depths or be gleaned from outside sources that are an enduring part of the human heritage. The sifting process usually brings with it a change of attitude. It invites a reordering of values. It often prompts a turn toward the sacred.

"I learned," people sometimes say, "that no one is going to take care of me except me, so I better get busy." We see others proclaim their utter helplessness and completely change their lives through a deep surrender to a higher power.

Process 3: Reconstructing

In this process, wisdom begins to take on a concrete form. The rubble is moved aside, and the future begins anew, grounded upon a few surviving values. They are cleaned up, polished, given more balance, then put back to work as the sun rises on a new day.

People start over. They move. They clear up their debts. They simplify life, start their own businesses, learn to love one another. Family members decide to try harder, to be less critical. Marriages once thought dead come back to life.

The concreteness of reconstructing becomes internalized in a more authentic self. Continuity from one day to the next flows from this new internal construction. A beginning wisdom turns to positive energy, and life begins moving again.

Process 4: Reintegrating

In this process, we note a significant shift from reliance upon external sources to a new trust of the self. The strengthened self begins to take a more active role, functioning as an internal guidance system. We call it the true self.

The self also begins to open up into a higher consciousness. It forms a compassionate connection with others. The person begins to transcend the limits of life and the discomfort of change. Life is then built upon foundations that last, and these flow from within. Wisdom deepens.

The banality and the ambiguity of life are now viewed differently. The person gains resiliency and flexibility, since life is governed by higher laws and deeper values. Future change is evaluated as inevitable.

This lifting of the human spirit touches the realm of the sacred, and we now speak of a developing spirituality. A formed and informed spirituality becomes more real, and as it matures, the person trusts it more deeply. Trust is grounded in intuition.

⫿ Process 5: Transcendence ⫿

Direction from the true self becomes central to living. Decisions are made and directions are sought by accessing a reservoir of rich wisdom. Life continues to change, but change becomes less threatening. Persons evolve more freely. They trust themselves. They trust their higher consciousness. They trust their relationship with the God Who is Wisdom. A spirituality matures, then gradually governs every dimension of life. Within this context, they reauthor the story of their lives.

⫿ Notes About Process ⫿

An explication of these five processes forms the core of this book. The remaining chapters will simply explore them at greater depth. We will suggest a number of *ways,* or *paths to wisdom,* as the chapters unfold, but present them only as stories or illustrations that are prototypal in nature. In other words, they act as models, and are written to open up your heart and your mind. No one path is to be taken as the definitive way to deeper wisdom. We leave the final selection of the most appropriate way to you, realizing that any well-integrated path to maturity involves serious study and commitment.

Our task is to present five dynamic processes and help you incorporate them into a more satisfying experience of living. The processes can be applied to any era of change or growth: early adulthood, midlife, or the later years.

Not every one, of course, moves through these processes in the same sequence. Styles vary immensely for men and women as they balance out masculine and feminine energies even within themselves. Each story is different. The challenges vary with the appropriate stages of adult development. There is no right or wrong way to evolve through them.

Some sojourners remain stuck in the initial process and never seem to right their lives or make them any better. Others soar like a red-tailed hawk, riding the summer thermals with inner composure and deep trust.

The essential attitude governing the transition from a disintegrated position to a mature spirituality is *openness*. You must be sufficiently open-minded and open-hearted to listen to what wiser voices are saying to you. If you develop this quality of openness, you can view almost any experience of change as an invitation to open up life to a new level of fulfillment.

Change is no stranger to the planet. Although our present context is unique in the history of the world, countless others before you have faced the proposition of change and survived. There is a collected wisdom in the human race that can help make sense out of life and offer a foundation for beginning all over again.

2.

DISINTEGRATION

The Ashes of Change

When life goes well, when purpose and meaning govern the daily agenda, positive energy flows freely. Activities are meaningful and fulfilling. Wisdom seems assured.

Insert unwelcome change into the agenda, however, and energy flags. New questions bubble to the surface of awareness, giving distinct form to the panic within.

"Which way do I turn?" people ask. "Where do I go for help? What is disposable in my life and what is salvageable? Which way am I to turn for direction and strength? What can I really believe? What is no longer viable for me?"

The questions touch every level of life, every component of the self. In order to initially explore the actuality of change, we will describe it as impacting on three levels: the defined structures of life, the collapse of fantasy, and the emotional consequences of change. Although the varieties of loss can be significant and widespread, we will describe only a few of them.

‖ Level One Losses: The Defined Structures of Life ‖

The Loss of Identity

"It happened so quickly," he reiterated several times. "I was really in a good position. Vice president of marketing for the entire company. When I walked through the corporate office doors, people called me 'Mr. Smith,' not John. I really enjoyed the prestige and the perks that came with the territory. Every year, I personally conducted tours to foreign countries to reward my top sales and marketing people for a job well done. That vice presidency was my life."

He paused in his narration, then breathed deeply several times as he assessed his audience: displaced male executives gathering once again for their support group. They listened attentively, undoubtedly feeling a consonance with their own stories.

"After getting forced out of my upper management position, I became a general agent, and now spend my days marketing life insurance policies. I hate it," he said, swallowing hard. "I don't believe in what I do or even what I sell. It takes enormous effort to get on the phone each morning and sound enthused about these products. I still dream about the days when I was a somebody. It's a good thing my wife has a respectable legal assistant's job, or we would probably starve to death."

The bitter disappointment described by this former executive evokes a haunting image of life taking a surprisingly cruel turn. No longer able to claim his identity from a perch high on the corporate ladder, he dropped into the nightmarish world of deep regrets, empty dreams, and isolation. His emptiness haunts him throughout the day. He dreams about his losses at night.

The difficult task of constructing an identity upon

something more solid than an organizational structure has presented to him a task he would rather not assume. For the moment, he finds little value in his life. His emptiness, however, is inviting him to look for a deeper source of a genuine self. Even though the invitation is clear, the task is not easy.

The Loss of Family Ties

"You can't believe what my family is doing to me over this thing," she related, looking pale and fatigued. Her marriage witnessed a successive series of abusive incidents, beginning with her first date with him. Even then, she was not strong enough to break out of his control.

Fifteen years later, his heavy drinking, unexplained nights out, degrading language, deplorable job performance, and a litany of other abusive behaviors dominate her marriage. Her parents help them with a monthly financial supplement, then deny any real problems when she shares her concerns.

"Their minimizing of my situation makes my life even more difficult," she explained. "They support him financially, but they aren't straight with me. The only reason they maintain the financial assistance is to make sure we stay married, so divorce won't tarnish their image.

"I got myself to the place where I knew I could no longer live this way," she reflected. "I filed for divorce. The papers were served; then the ripple effects of my action moved through my family like you wouldn't believe. They accuse me of being crazy and insist that I 'back off.' They tell me I am unfair to him. They threaten me with loss of income. They even say they will disown me if I go through with the divorce."

The day the divorce papers were served, her husband

experienced an instant conversion, vowing never to drink again. He joined not one, but three AA groups. He became visibly theatrical about his new behavior, especially in front of her family. In turn, they quizzed her scrupulously about her disloyalty to him. The pressure mounted for several months.

"They just won't let go of me," she said one day when her emptiness pressed in upon her. "I'm not so sure I can follow through with this. Now they're even threatening to take my kids away from me."

As we observe so often in complicated domestic problems, these situations bring with them a terrible agony. In some cases, the only resolution is to make hard decisions to move on, even at the risk of breaking family ties.

The superhuman effort demanded by this woman has brought her to the threshold of a more genuine self. She is, at last, prepared to move on with her life and make it work. For the first time since they met, she is free of her husband's intimidation and control. Even though the potential losses are high, she is willing to pay a heavy price for her peace of mind.

The Loss of Direction

Life changes for every person, and when it does, it brings with it at least a temporary loss of direction.

"You've got to help us," came the plea one afternoon. The soft, yet firm voice on the other end of the phone connection brought us to attention.

"Help you what?" we asked.

"Help us deal with the closing of our motherhouse. We are at the place in our province where we can no longer afford to keep the motherhouse open. We sisters have such a hard time dealing with that. No one really wants to talk about it, and the stresses within the order are very strong."

We simply listened for a time, interspersing our concern for their predicament with a few questions about the specifics of their situation.

"We are now forced to completely shut down our motherhouse," she continued, breathing a little more quickly. "It is a symbol of all that we are as a province. Most of the sisters began their relationship with our order in that home. They trained there. They come back home for days of renewal. It still remains home for so many of us. Now we have to close it down." Her account trailed off into an uncomfortable silence.

We could feel the tension again as her voice strengthened. "Let me assure you," she insisted, "we are facing enormous changes, and none of the sisters want to deal with their feelings. We feel a profound loss of direction and we need the two of you to help us find our way. We simply can't talk. We end up angry and distant every time we meet as a group."

The changes she described now forced a complete reevaluation of everything the sisters had associated with religious life: living arrangements, the meaning of a supportive community, long-term care of infirm members, and now their very future. In brief, a whole value system continued collapsing around them, and they were unable to creatively dialogue about it or problem-solve.

The loss of direction is shared by every member, and the leadership hard-pressed to help them find their way through the reality of change. The province remains inundated with deep questions about loss, emptiness, and even a future. It became clear from our initial contact that a long struggle lay ahead of them. We knew we could be witnessing the end of a way of life.

The Loss of Confidence

"Jim and I really do love each other," she insisted. "We began our relationship when both our lives fell apart through divorces.

"I just don't know whether we can find the energy it takes to keep this family together," she sighed. "There is so much conflict in our lives. His teenagers are the most difficult. I swear they have a conspiracy against me. They pick away at me, especially when Jim is not around. They make my life so miserable. By the time he comes home from work, I am in tears, and when I explain my emptiness to him, he doesn't really listen to me. He thinks I'm overreacting to his kids, and he tells me that if I would 'lighten up a bit' the situation could be so much better. The meals in silence, the long nights of not talking to one another—even the emptiness I carry—are so bad."

She had a hard time telling her story. Her hopes for a happy marriage held up for a few short weeks before disappearing under a heavy cloud of tension and conflict. Her therapist simply listened with compassion, being cautious not to suggest a simplistic answer to a complex situation.

"I would give anything—anything—to get back that idyllic time when Jim and I could be so supportive of one another," she said. "Now when we do have time alone, it seems like the conflicts with the children contaminate our ability to see and hear each other clearly."

A loss of confidence in her ability to make love work has left a deep vacuum in this woman's life, and there will be no easy reclaiming it. She finds little help from those who encourage her to let go of her dreams, then start all over again as a single person. As she struggles to find some ways to reclaim her lost confidence, only her therapist's encouragement sustains her.

Losses at this first level of change are the easiest to describe, for they are measured by the collapse of tangible realities, interpersonal relationships, and predictable structures. In many of these situations, the reconstructing of life involves nothing more than the substitution of one concrete goal for another. The change may or may not bring with it an engendered wisdom, but it does invite the person to look at life more critically. A deeper wisdom usually evolves after the deeper structures of life collapse, and they often do so because they are made of empty dreams.

Level Two Losses:
The Collapse of Fantasy

Fantasies form a fragile yet common foundation for life, and their collapse brings with them a genuine emptiness. Their magnitude is a reflection of the unbridgeable gap that exists between unrealistic goals, unattainable dreams, deep longings of the heart, and the realities of life.

Innumerable fantasies inhabit the human imagination. It would be impossible to reflect upon them at any depth in a short book. We have discovered three, however, that are especially problematic.

Fantasy 1:

Someone Is Going to Rescue Me from the Hard Reality of Life
"It took me three failed marriages to discover that my fantasy of the perfect woman does not exist," he said blandly. The curtain rose on his current drama the afternoon he returned to his upscale apartment to find every stick of furniture cleaned out. A simple note from his wife occupied the space usually reserved for his favorite

Gorman. Her typed, cryptic message informed him that he would be hearing from her attorney.

"She did her best," he sighed, "but it just wasn't enough to make me happy. She finally walked out on me after telling me so many times to get a life of my own. It really doesn't surprise me in a way," he said, "since I've spent most of my thirty-two years looking for the perfect mate. I wanted someone who would love me unconditionally."

His family background was stiff, formal, and unexpressive. He remembered his mother as a detached and distant figure, who was always too busy to spend time with him. Consequently, he lived most of his life hungering for a nurturing love to fill up his emptiness.

His quest for the perfect love met with continued disappointment. Every time he found a hint of love in his life, he would either test it to the limit, or completely dismantle it by claiming it was not enough to satisfy him. He exhausted a number of women through this cycle of hunger and rejection, easily scuttling three marriages.

"This time I'm ready to look at myself," he said as his tears welled up. "It looks like I have been looking in the wrong place for too long. It just hasn't worked. I still feel empty, and I better find out why this emptiness won't leave. I finally have to admit to myself that no one is going to love me enough to make the pain go away."

Fantasies of the perfect mate usually die hard, leaving enormous emptiness in the wake of their collapse. The hard work of learning to love can be taxing, but a shared life will never last unless it is built upon more realistic expectations. The beginning of wisdom is to understand that no one can love us so selflessly that we will never again feel empty or afraid. The emptiness is also an invitation to the male to discover feminine energy deep within the self. In doing so, he learns to nurture himself, rather than expecting a woman to rescue him from his emptiness. No matter what the gender questions, however, no one is going to rescue us.

Fantasy 2:
The Stars (or God) Will Rescue Me, No Matter What I Do

"I prayed like I never prayed before," he said. "They're closing in on me. My creditors know I'm not being straight with them about their money, and they want an accounting.

"If God deals in miracles," he asked, "why doesn't he give me one now? I read in this book about miracles that if you pray with good faith and really trust, God will grant one. It hasn't come yet. My pastor told me to pray like I've never prayed before. So I do. I was awake all last night, praying my heart out."

He labored over his description, and for good reason. He made his living managing a number of investment accounts, but he had grossly mismanaged his clients' money. Worse yet, he used their money for his own purposes, intending to replace it when a few speculative ventures paid off. The ventures never jelled, and the day of reckoning had arrived. The accounts were dry. As he told his story, he hyperventilated briefly, then regained his composure. In the shadows of his awareness lurked the specter of a prison sentence.

The only messengers descending upon him to date were his angry clients, but they brought no heavenly greetings with them, only their attorneys. God was nowhere to be found.

This book is not about miracles, but it does explore the notion of spirituality. More specifically, it is about an adult spirituality. This grade of spirituality begins with the realities of life, not a rescue fantasy. It faces the challenges of life squarely and honestly, applying the gifts of problem-solving, genuine creativity, and honesty, acknowledging them as gifts that are already given by a generous God.

Indeed, miracles do happen at times, but they are usually unexpected, reflecting God's design rather than our feeble efforts at damage control. To refuse to take responsibility for our lives, then expect the stars or the loving God to rescue us, is to look in the wrong places.

Fantasy 3:
You Will Achieve Every One of Your Dreams

"I dreamed we could live out our years together, then retire and have a little place by the lake to really enjoy a more leisurely pace," he said. "We built our little place all right, then this thing hit me, and it has been unbearable. She moved out and told me I better get over my anger before she moves back in."

He looked straight ahead into his own darkness as he talked.

"It just doesn't make any sense," he said, "to work this hard for sixty years and then end up blind like this. I might as well be living in an apartment in the inner city. I can't see the beauty of this place. I can't do anything. I have no way out."

Not all stories of unfulfilled dreams are as harsh as this one, but they do express one reality: all of our dreams will not be fulfilled. Life is life, not a romantic tale of undisturbed bliss.

Dreams of a bigger home, more freedom, more toys, greater mobility, a stress-free retirement, or endless days in the sun at a perfect hideaway, seldom materialize. The perfect vacation ends in a week of rain and cold; a romantic night out crashes with mixed-up reservations. The love boat stalls in mid-ocean with major maintenance problems.

Like the man gone prematurely blind, the unpredictability of life can be a source of deep darkness and crusty hostility, making it miserable for our self as well as for everyone around us.

Sometimes the beginning of wisdom is the simple acceptance that some of our dreams will remain unfulfilled, but that must not allow us to become cynical or hopelessly angry.

As we listen to people tell their stories about how their lives have dramatically changed, we hear about other fantasies that have collapsed. Their telling offers a commentary on how much life has changed in America. Here are a few of the maxims American people once believed:

If you work hard, you will get ahead.
Loyalty on the job will bring its own rewards.
I will be able to maintain my middle class life for as
    long as I choose.
You take good care of the company, and the company
    will take good care of you.
If you are vulnerable and open, love will blossom.
Hard work, honesty, and creativity will open the door
    to anything you want.

The sobering fact of collapsed fantasy brings a person face to face with what is real and what is the product of an overly-zealous imagination. The collapse also invites a critical examination of the foundations for an authentic life and a mature spirituality. "Is the universe a friendly place?" people ask with impassioned curiosity. "Is there a destiny written in the stars? Is God for real? Is there such a thing as a relationship with God? Or has everything in my life collapsed in bitter disappointment?"

For many, only the stars hold the answer.

Level Three Losses: The Emotional Context

Like us, human development theorist William Bridges spent many years studying the reactions of people confronted with unwanted and widespread change: interpersonal, organizational, familial, and individual. As he monitored their transitions, he uncovered a number of predictable emotional reactions that characterize each change. Likewise, he discovered that the person's ability to deal with these reactions will determine their future success or failure. He terms their predictable emotional reactions, *signs of grieving.*[1]

1. Denial. This reaction represents the person's first and often unconscious effort to protect him-or herself from the pain of loss.
2. Anger. This emotion expresses a broad spectrum of reactions, from grumbling to rage. Anger can be directed at a legitimate source or misdirected at whoever might be a "lightning rod" for the discharge. It can take the forms of overt expression, foot-dragging, "mistakes," or sabotage.
3. Bargaining. This internal process is an effort to hold back the onslaught of change, make a deal, offer unrealistic promises, or make other efforts to postpone the inevitable.
4. Sadness is the heart of the grieving process. It is usually expressed in reactions that range from grim silence,

through a pervasive gloom that refuses to lift, to mad ravings about injustice in the system.

5. Disorientation describes a state characterized by feelings of loss and insecurity. All surroundings become vague and unfamiliar. It can be manifested in confusion and forgetfulness, even among ordinarily disciplined and conscientious people.

6. Depression. This is a persistent feeling of being down, flat, dead, hopeless, and demoralized. Some complain that they feel tired all the time.

7. Anxiety is a reaction to an unknown or difficult future. Fantasies of impending catastrophe are a common expression. Anxiety can be silent or expressed.

Negative Anger, Positive Anger

Each person is unique. Each story of coping with change is nuanced by uncountable variations and attitudes. Therefore, any one of these signs of grieving can represent a focus for unprecedented personal growth, or a place for incipient developmental processes to become hopelessly stuck. Anger will serve as an example of what we mean.

Like Bridges, we see anger working within the experience of change. If it is turned inward, the end product can be an ever-deepening sadness and corrosive cynicism about the merciless and unfeeling events of life. It can lead to a *stuck* position that totally immobilizes. Feelings of deep and relentless despair are often charged by an unbending anger at one's self, for judging so badly or acting so poorly. Consequently, anger actually intensifies the despair. We sometimes refer to this and other dysfunctional variations on anger as *negative anger*.

Anger can also be a beautifully freeing emotion when it is focused on new goals. We call this *positive anger*. For many, it forms the bedrock of change, and begins to reorient the entire emotional life of the person toward the reconstruction of new dreams. Positive anger also mobilizes other emotions that are useful in the task of reconstruction. It provides the energy needed to get life going again.

Julia Cameron, in her reflections on intuition, equates the use of anger with the recovery of personal power:

> Anger is meant to be listened to. Anger is a voice, a shout, a plea, a demand. Anger is meant to be respected. Why? Because anger is a *map*. Anger shows us what our boundaries are. Anger shows us where we want to go. It lets us see where we've been and lets us know when we haven't liked it. Anger points the way, not just the finger. In the recovery of a blocked artist, anger is the sign of health....With a little thought, we can usually translate the message that our anger is sending us.[2]

An example will help illustrate what we mean by positive anger.

"At first, I received the news pretty casually," he stated. His listeners nodded in support of his bravado. They now bonded in a solidarity that the faxed notice of termination was a genuine affront to everything they ever affirmed about the proper way to do business.

"I even half-believed that silly little flyer from the home office's public relations lackey," he continued. "The flyer informed us that the loss of our jobs is really an opportunity for new growth. The flyer went into this long explanation that the word *crisis* is the other side of opportunity, and loss is only a matter of weak attitudes. I tore it up into little pieces, really believing I was handling the situation very well by myself."

The group encouraged him to keep talking, visibly resonating with deep emotions as he described his final hours with the company.

"I had a dream a couple of nights later," he continued, pausing long enough to take another jolt of black coffee.

"I dreamed I was facing a dozen upper management types, all dressed in their five-hundred-dollar pinstripe suits and their silly-ass power ties. Their backs were against what looked like the Wrigley Field wall."

He became more animated as he continued. His lips thinned. His listeners came to attention. "I trotted onto the field from a dugout as the fans cheered for me," he said. "I was dressed in a camouflage military uniform and carried an assault rifle instead of a baseball bat. The faceless men in their gray suits just stared at me: no expression, no emotion. I reached down to my side for an ammunition clip, inserted it into my M-16, and opened up with full automatic on the whole group. The gun bucked and jumped and they dropped like flies. Blood all over the place."

He took his time before continuing, slowly wrapping his delicate hands, one long finger at a time, around the thick coffee mug. His listeners looked troubled, cautiously nodding at him to continue.

"Then I felt my anger changing to guilt over what I had done," he said, loosening his grip. "I looked down at my M-16 and discovered I had inserted a red copy toner cartridge into the firing chamber and had sprayed them with red ink. No real bullets, no real hurt, no real destruction. I felt relieved, but I was facing a whole line of executives who were madder than hell at me now. They started yelling and screaming about me about ruining their suits and ties. They were furious. So I pulled the empty toner cartridge out of my M-16, threw it at their feet, and walked away like Rambo saying, 'Fax me the cleaning bills.' Then I woke up in a cold sweat."

As tainted as this illustration is with potential violence, a deep core of anger helped this vulnerable man organize his capacity to make an important transition. His dream firmed up a resolution that he would never, ever again, give a group of nameless and faceless corporate executives this much control over his life. The anger not only mobilized his energy, it kept him focused on the development of a successful business of his own.

"Positive anger begins the process of change," we often say. "It can move you from a victim status to an active engagement with reality. Now you need to take some of that energy and organize it around the rediscovery of the wisdom that lies within you."

Thus we direct people on to the next task in their evolution: sifting for the latent wisdom that sleeps within them.

3.

SIFTING

Listening for a Voice Within

Sifting through the ashes of change and the discovery of latent wisdom are intimately connected. We sometimes refer to this process as *soul work:* a journey downward into the depths of the self to search for wisdom. To shed light on the psychological, emotional and spiritual processes involved in this task, we again turn to images of the federal building in Oklahoma City.

The rescue worker's arduous task is to sift through a mountain of rubble, one piece at a time, in order to find life. In this labor, a muffled cry for help, a photo, a teddy bear, or an I.D. card, become symbols of hope. Their discovery spurs the workers on to track each lead, explore every hope.

Even though we use the term *sifting* to characterize a number of internal processes, its labors can be as demanding as the physical rescue work we describe. It brings with it unique dramas of hope and despair, labor and reward, exhaustion and refreshment.

This woman's story will help you to understand what we mean:

"When my twenty-year marriage ended," she exclaimed, "I didn't think I was going to make it. Everything I ever hoped for or dreamed about came to an end, and I was totally devastated."

Her narration halted as she stumbled to find the right words, then she began to cry, lending spontaneous authenticity to her story.

"I was so depressed I couldn't function—I *didn't* function," she continued, "I slipped into such a sad case. Lost track of my friends. Spent all my time alone. I suffered through work, then would go home and cry into the night. I was absolutely miserable, angry at my ex-husband for all that he had done to me."

She stopped, then regained her composure after breathing deeply a few times. "I don't know what brought the turnaround in my life for sure," she said. "I think I just hit the place where I knew I would lose everything if I didn't act. It scared me, and my feelings pushed me to get organized again. Maybe my grieving was over—I don't know. But I do remember getting really angry, throwing things around my apartment and screaming at the four walls to my absent ex-husband, 'You might have killed our marriage, but you'll never kill my spirit!' From there on, I slowly started to put my life back together."

Like the rescue worker who celebrates the uncovering of a small toy, a picture, a letter, or a simple object that represents a significant breakthrough in his search for life, the discovery of deeper wisdom can flow from a deceptively small finding. The finding brings with it a new agenda: a surge of energy to continue digging, a reward for sustaining hope against overwhelming odds, the discovery of new life. The women often speak of rediscovering their deep feminine roots, their intuitive powers, or their legitimate place in a relationship. The men describe their tasks as opening up new options, or structuring life differently. Both feel positive about the discovery of their new foundations.

In this chapter, we will explore a number of these findings, gleaned from the stories of our work with many people. We will also describe some of the ways that these renewed sources of wisdom can open the way to new life for you. We refer to this process as "listening to the wisdom within."

Findings: A New Reason For Living

"I think the breakthrough came to me the night I weighed whether or not to go ahead with a heart transplant," the man said. "I had already been in the hospital for two weeks, trying to deal with myocardiopathy."

His language offered a solid clue to his background. He had spent most of his adult years practicing medicine as a capable and compassionate surgeon. At the peak of his career, deepening fatigue moved him to consult with a heart specialist who diagnosed his problem as a chronic and deadly heart disease—myocardiopathy.

The disease forced his early retirement. Several months later, a serious heart attack confined him to the coronary care unit. When the heart team weighed his options for treatment, only two were practicable: die of coronary artery disease within a year, or take a placement on the waiting list for a heart transplant.

"I thought about my options for several long days while I fought a deep depression," he said. "My life was turned completely upside down. I knew I was not going to get well on my own. The risks, pain, and relative merits of a heart transplant were very hard to deal with. My body could completely reject the donor heart, and I would die anyway. My emotions worked on me overtime. I was really scared. My decision boiled down to one hard question: was anything in my life worth the suffering associated with a heart transplant?

"Finally," he confessed after a thoughtful pause, "it came to this. I thought one night about my son and his wife, who were about to have another child. I decided right then and there I was going to go ahead with the transplant because a new grandchild is worth living for. Once I made the decision, I felt okay about it. The next day I told my physician to put my name on the list."

Sifting life down to bare essentials of what is worth living for or what is worth dying for, brings us face to face with profound truths. The sifting process not only focuses life on tangible goals, it fosters an alignment of the deep psychological and emotional components of the self. Energy is freed to invest in a creative response to life. Inner clarity is expressed in a new decisiveness. Clearheadedness and peacefulness become wisdom's reward.

Findings: A New Independence

"I really believed that if I married him, I would never have to worry about my isolation again. I knew he would be unswervingly loyal to me in every situation. I would never want for love and attention." She paused momentarily, looked puzzled, then confessed. "But I was wrong. I was simply wrong."

Her husband's deep sensitivity to her every need dried up in their first six months together, leaving her puzzled and empty. He never said a word about what was going on with him.

"He just disappears for long periods of time and leaves

me alone," she continued. "He doesn't consult with me; he doesn't ask me my opinion. Apparently, he just assumes I'll be fine, and I feel terribly abandoned and empty."

Even though the evolution of her life had not proceeded as expected, her story remained that of self-discovery, not despair. At the basis of this discovery lay a major change in the structure of her life: a shift away from an other-orientation to a clearly defined self-direction.

"His notable absence and my disappointment about it finally forced me to look at myself," she continued. "After endless nights of crying myself to sleep, I finally admitted that he is not interested in rescuing me from my loneliness. It looks like I'll have to work on that one myself. This time I'm determined to do something about it."

Like the rescue workers who overcome fatigue, sadness, boredom, and routine in their search for life in the tangled debris, the most surprising and difficult shifts in life-orientation can stimulate extraordinary desires to be whole.

Ⅱ Findings: Small Matters of Hope Ⅱ

"Blending a family has got to be the most difficult thing we have ever tried to do," he said. "At the beginning, it looked like we would all fit together so well. Julie and I did weekends together, laughed and enjoyed one another's company. We looked forward to a time when the marriage would finally be in place."

Phil sat alone with us. His emptiness was apparent, registered in the deep worry lines of his face. Julie was absent. She moved back to her home town in a definitive effort to reclaim her personal space. Her teenage sons went with her. Phil's teenage daughter remained with him in their new home. The young marriage had been blown apart by the relentless tension between hostile segments in the family, and the alienation was not likely to lift for a time.

"This is my third effort to make marriage work," he said sadly. "Obviously it has not gone the way I antici-pated. Julie and I still love one another and we are clear about that, but we just don't do very well living under the same roof. We end up yelling at each other about parent-ing, about this, about that, about who is responsible for what. It got so bad we had to separate."

Phil sifted for several hours that day, weighing the value of their love, the pros and cons of staying together, and the possibility of divorce. His findings were inconclu-sive. At the end of several hours of hard work, he was more focused on a positive direction than when he began.

"I guess it comes to this," he said thoughtfully. "There is one thing that Julie and I both hold on to. We still believe in one another and deeply desire to make this thing work. So we'll go back to the drawing board to see if we can reconstruct it. She has agreed to come pay you a visit next week and talk about this mess from her perspective."

Like a lonely beacon marking the edges of a treacher-ous coastline on the darkest of nights, the human spirit can be sustained, focused, and directed by the smallest glim-mer of hope.

ǁ Findings: Trusting One's Self ǁ

"I know I should have trusted myself from the very beginning," she stated. Her manner conveyed a mixture of sorrow and firm determination to change her life.

"He turned out to be very manipulative, very conniving, and I tried so hard to please him that I lost track of who I am for far too long."

She spoke haltingly, searching for the proper words to convey the hard task of the last several years. Her presence was striking, manifesting an inner beauty that comes only through struggle and hard resolve.

"He is a very verbal person," she related. "He talks circles around me. I try to express myself, but he defines reality right out from under me; then I get confused. I suppose my biggest motivation from the very beginning was to try to please him. In order to do so, I made far too many concessions.

"It was so bad," she continued. "If I didn't do things his way, he would punish me with distance and indifference, then I would weaken and apologize for everything I did wrong. He always made himself look good. I looked like the one who was unhappy.

"All the time I was so compliant," she said with deepening intensity. "I tried hard to be the dutiful wife, while he carried on an affair with his secretary. When I finally woke up to what was going on with him, I really lost it. I threw him out of the house. Then he kept asking me how I could be so unreasonable. That really infuriated me, especially since this affair had rolled on for five years.

"Never!" she said, her eyes narrowing. "Never will I let another male define who I am. I knew it was wrong for me from the very beginning and I should have trusted myself, but I kept quiet in order to keep him happy. Now I know what a degrading and manipulative game I bought into, and it will never happen again.

"It took me five full years of hard work," she reiterated, "to come full circle to what I should have done in the first place: trust myself. This time my trust is for keeps."

As we often discover in marital situations like this, deep changes unfold when a person reclaims values, attitudes, and dreams that bring them full circle to a genuine trust of themselves. Their intuition told them their early decisions were weak, but they ignored their inner voice. Now the same voice jolts them into an awareness that they have within them all they need to make life work, but they must learn to trust it. We usually speak of this process as, "recovering your core essence."

ǁ Sifting: Listening to the Power of the Generations ǁ

"I never fully appreciated where my tenacity comes from until now," she said. "I know it is always there, like a reservoir of strength when I need it, but it took the collapse of a marriage for me to understand how deep that reservoir really is."

Her ex-husband had already moved to another state, leaving the family on its own. Child support for their three children arrived late, if it arrived at all. Although she remained composed as she told her story, she left no doubt about her awareness of the challenges that lay ahead of her.

"I think I gained my strength through the generations," she reflected. "My great grandparents were German immigrants who moved westward with the settlement of the Dakota Territory. They had a hard life, opening up the prairie to the new agriculture. My grandparents and parents continued their legacy of hard work and honesty right on through the Great Depression. I remember my dad telling stories about life in South Dakota during the dust bowl of the thirties. The drifting topsoil piled up around the fence posts like snow in a January blizzard. The whole sky blew dirty red from horizon to horizon. When the rains finally came, it rained mud for two days straight. The skies no sooner cleared than the locusts arrived, eating everything in sight, even the fence posts. Many people despaired. They left twenty or thirty years of hard work behind them, moving on to find a better life, but my family stayed and fought. Now both my parents are gone, but I grew up with the notion that you stay and fight rather than give up. My stubbornness is clearly a generational thing."

Deep within the self lie sources for starting all over again that represent a synthesis of unspoken gifts given by previous generations. This legacy can go unnoticed during periods of routine living, then come to life when a major change demands a deeper resourcefulness. The gifts then evolve into a contemporary expression of tenacity.

In her book *Dakota: A Spiritual Geography,* Kathleen Norris speaks of this gift as the Plains legacy. She pays special tribute to the women:

> To learn the truth about the web of close-knit families that make up an isolated small town on the Plains, one must look back some years, to the men and women of the homesteading and early merchant generation. By now they've mostly been mythologized into the stern, hard-working papa and the over-worked-mother-who-never-complained, all their passions and complexities smoothed over. But many of these people, the women especially, had an intense love/hate relationship with the Plains that lives on in their children. Some mourned the loss of European culture or ethnic roots; others, the social status they'd enjoyed in the cities back East. Only the toughest survived here.[3]

ǀǀ Findings: The Spirit That Refuses to Die ǀǀ

The time is 1993, deep in the summer of the great midwestern flood. It rained incessantly during the spring months, and now vast areas of America's heartland wash away at the mercy of raging streams and rivers. The rampage evolves into the most widespread flooding in American history. The displaced and the homeless ask for help. Their plea is amplified through a general call from the disaster relief services for more volunteers. Within a day we find ourselves working at a neighborhood food distribution site.

It is located within a short walk of the river bottoms, near an area hardest hit by the flood. The site, traditionally peppered with low income housing, is left scoured and sculpted by roiling water. The neighbors seek to reclaim their territory, working hard to rescue a few possessions from the muddy waters, silt, and smelly sludge. Under the oppression of relentless July heat, they patiently wait for the arrival of the Red Cross ERV—the emergency response vehicle. We arrive on schedule and set up the ERV for a day of food distribution.

Mothers, flanked by their clingy grade-schoolers, shift their babies from one hip to another while they wait in line for food. We begin distributing meals of hot Irish stew, heavy bread, boiled vegetables, and iced lemonade.

"Can I take four meals?" one man asks, "I have a sick brother and a couple of kids back at the house, and there's no food, just a basement full of water."

"Yessir," a Red Cross volunteer answers, "take all you want. There is no shortage here." The man nods in appreciation, then quickly turns toward home, beaming over his treasures.

The weather changes frequently, alternating between

oppressively humid heat and heavy downpours. The sun returns to bake the parking lot into a sticky swamp. The back end of the ERV turns into a steam cooker. We all sweat, laboring to get the food out while doing our best to maintain sanitary conditions. Our hands stay drenched in pesky beads of perspiration, collecting inside our plastic food-handler gauntlets. We alternate shifts at the food tables, then step out of the ERV to breathe less humid air. Talk with the neighborhood people comes easily.

"I'm out of work for at least three weeks at Montfort Packing Company," a man relates, "and I have a wife and two little ones at home, which is a mess. I can't go back to work until the water supply is restored, 'cause they can't process fresh beef with contaminated water. Another week out of work and I won't be able to pay my rent."

A woman approaches us with a question. "I have two elderly heart patients at home with me," she says innocently, "my mother and my aunt, and they depend on me for food. I hope you people keep coming to this place or I can't take care of them. We can't afford any other kind of care."

We assure her we'll do our best, all the while working to keep our composure. This litany of human suffering is difficult to hear, especially when it contrasts so strongly with the abundance of this city.

The sun breaks out again. The children respond to the brightness by donning oversize red, green, or yellow sun glasses. The fluorescent glasses dwarf their small faces, but cannot dim their bright smiles.

A Southeast Asian woman gestures frantically to break the language barrier. "Would it be all right," she asks, "to come each day to the distribution site and take home enough food for the three elderly persons I care for?"

We reassure her again that there will be no food shortage and encourage her to be sure to ask for all she wants.

It starts raining again. The downpour becomes oppressive within two minutes, rocking and pounding the ERV, before elevating the humidity toward the century mark. The temperature is nearly there already. The volunteers sweat profusely, look skyward, then shake their heads in disbelief.

"Why," a woman rasps, "must the rains continue? If God loves the poor so much, why don't they ever get a break? They are always the most vulnerable. They can't escape this business like those who flew out to cool and dry vacation spots."

The long lines form again. The rain tantalizes us with a diminishing beat, then an ominous sky opens up and unloads heavy winds and horizontal sheets of water that pummel us for a solid hour. Those in line brave the cold rain for awhile, then it becomes too much for them. Several of us working outside the van get soaked, but we no longer care. We can't get any wetter. We communicate with other brave souls who hold boxes, papers, umbrellas, jackets, and garbage bags over their heads in a futile effort to stay dry. Undaunted, the neighborhood people trek back in singles and doubles for their evening meal: roast turkey, mashed potatoes, dressing and gravy.

Getting soaked, talking freely, helping the handicapped carry food to their cars, laughing at the weather, all take on a cleansing value. Every trace of racial, ethnic, or cultural difference among the assembled is washed clean. We erupt in laughter at times at the sheer joy of being alive. The rain becomes a baptism into the solidarity of the human spirit that refuses to die.

The collective spirit that carried these neighborhood

people through one more adversity is a powerful one. None of them was a stranger to hard experiences. They learned early in their lives that life is a difficult proposition, and they know they are called upon once again to move on in spite of oppressive circumstances.

This tenacious spirit continued to haunt us after the waters receded and we completed our work. We wrestled with it, trying to identify what it was that sustained so many of those with whom we conversed. Perhaps it was the same spirit that Susan L. Taylor named for her people. In her opus, *In the Spirit,* she describes a spirit that haunted her as she stood alone on a beach in Ghana. There she surveyed the old slave pens, while praying for the unidentified millions who were exported from that precise location into a life of slavery:

> ...I learned that most of the Africans taken into slavery were very young. The children and young adults were captured in the outlying regions and herded to the shore....I wanted to pray at the places where they had walked in shackles to canoes waiting to shuttle them to the slave ships....It is difficult to comprehend the misery that our ancestors endured and survived. What they overcame....The wonder is not that so many perished, but that so many survived. The survival of our ancestors who lived through the Middle Passage and through the horrors of slavery is a story of the triumph of the spirit, the power of the divine.[4]

The legacy of strength in the midst of hard times lives on, and we often see a fresh manifestation of this spirit when change settles in. It sustains people with a quiet dignity. Its presence can be contagious.

ǁ Findings: Compassion for the Self ǁ

"I spent most of my life criticizing myself for not being perfect," she disclosed. "I agonized over my own mistakes, worried if I measured up to my own high standards. It took me a long time to figure out why I am so miserable." As she talked, she surveyed the remains of another failed marriage. It had lasted two years.

"My husband walked out on me because he said he could no longer stand being around me. He told me my ideals are too high, that I always expect perfection—not only for myself but for him as well. I know he's right, but it's too late now to salvage anything. He's gone."

Her emptiness showed in her manner, and for the first time in several months she began to cry. She talked between sobs. "I have reached the end of the line," she continued. "I'm just so tired of failure, of living up to my own impossibly high standards."

In the months that followed, she began a serious process of sifting in psychotherapy, searching for the compassionate response toward herself that had eluded her for a lifetime. Her desire for wholeness quickened her self-discovery. She learned that her perfectionism began through the love and approval measured out by her parents, if she performed well. Every relationship from there on became tainted with her continued need for approval. She placed high demands upon herself in order to be accepted by others. She could only accept herself if it represented a reward for a job well done. Her rigidity never allowed her to enjoy good friends or carefree conversation.

Even though an awareness about the roots of her rigidity developed rather easily, she moved more slowly toward an honest and comfortable self-affirmation. Old patterns of self-criticism resisted change. Finally, at age forty, she began to take the first steps to be compassionate toward herself. Once she took a few initial steps, the resistance crumbled under the emergence of newly discovered freedom. She learned to forgive herself. She even began to enjoy her own company. The energy that once drove her to harsh self-criticism now refocused on creativity. For the first time in her life she felt free, savoring the rewards that flow from the development of compassion.

Christina Feldman and Jack Kornfield describe the unique quality of compassion in this way:

> Compassion is that singular quality of heart that has the power to transform resentment into forgiveness, hatred into friendliness, anger into loving-kindness. It is the most precious quality of our being that allows us to extend warmth, sensitivity, and openness to the world around us and to ourselves rather than being burdened by prejudice, hostility, and resistance.[5]

The discovery of compassion brings with it an engaging wisdom. It not only softens the hardness toward ourselves, it opens out toward a genuine care for others. The discovery brings with it another bonus: relationships begin working for the first time.

Findings: Tapping the Reservoir of Creativity

"I knew I was dead-ended," he said. "I hated to get out of bed in the morning to go to work because my job was so boring. I wanted to quit a hundred times, but the timing was never right. So I went through the motions of living for another ten years, letting my life slip by, day by boring day, while I let it consume me. I'll admit it; I was hopelessly trapped by the golden handcuffs of state government. I was literally surrounded by people like myself who had gone to work for the state in order to retire."

He smiled about the irony of what had happened to him. "I became another forlorn casualty of governmental reorganization," he laughed. "The governor kept telling the voters he was saving all this taxpayers' money by combining departments, but I knew that he was making a big deal out of nothing. He shifted a few departments here and there while we all remained bored to death, looking for something to do. I sat next to a guy who spent his entire day reading fishing magazines while he waited for an assignment from his department head. As far as I know, he's still waiting for it, happily reading away."

He smiled again, looking genuinely content. "That was the end for me," he said. "They offered me a lateral move to another empty shell job, so I refused. They forced me out and I knew it. That night my wife and I drank a whole bottle of wine, and we rejoiced together that I was free at last. I started my own consulting business the next week, and it has been an unbelievably successful venture. Now I wish I had made that move ten years ago."

The revitalization of this bored government employee came during a moment of truth in his life: he was victimized by the myth of security and fulfillment. His sifting for a new reality brought with it an opening up of the most productive period of his life. The change came when he listened to the voice within him about his undeveloped creativity.

∥ Sifting and Consolidating ∥

As we listen to stories about the pressures and prompt-ings of the many voices within, we marvel at the diversity of the fonts underlying the emergence of a vital wisdom. Some are easily identified; some possess no name. It matters little if we can identify them, however, for they all bring with them the gifts associated with the embrace of a new vision.

A slight shift in attitude, a fresh desire for success, a compassionate embrace of one's own person, a release of sadness, a movement toward forgiveness—all invite the awakening of a new experience of living. Vital energy comes to life in the grounding, alignment, and guidance offered through an encounter with new wisdom. Naming the specific sources matters little. What matters is how cre-atively the new wisdom is integrated into a successful life.

Sifting demands the discipline to stop running from your restlessness and to discover what it means to listen. This is not an easy task, especially in a society that invites continual distraction and chronic busyness.

We suggest a simple beginning exercise to assist you with the sifting process:

1. Take some quiet reflective time and put your creativity to work. Imagine yourself carried aloft on the wings of an eagle. From there, you discover a rich new perspec-tive on your life. Major decisions at critical times in your history are now visible before you: your memorable suc-cesses, passages from one stage of life to another, your proud accomplishments. This panoramic view from above helps you to place your present endeavors within the context of an entire lifetime of successes and failures.
2. Now examine the successes in your life. Try to identify the practical wisdom that carries you from one era to

another. Is its source unknown? Is it a deeply-held value that still undergirds your goals and dreams? Is it the power and wisdom of the generations flowing in your blood? Is it a sincere belief in your capacity to make life work? Is it faith in God? Is it anger that pushes you to no longer feel beaten? Is it a vision that keeps you focused on an optimistic future? Whatever this sustaining wisdom might be, see if you can give form and definition to it. If you are unable to name it at the moment, can you accept the fact that its energy is real? Can you learn to trust it?

3. Reflect on this reality: if this wisdom has carried you this far in life without fail, why would it not be reliable for the continuation of your life? Can you learn to trust it now?

4. If obstacles need to be moved out of the way to make this wisdom even more functional for you, what are they? Worn out beliefs that no longer fit the context of your life? Denial that you have the capacity to think more creatively? Stubborn fears that impede success? A belief that success is too good to be true? Fear of the unknown? These are rather common obstacles to real changes in life, but if they are owned and examined critically, they can be moved out of the way.

5. Now make one resolution about tapping your unused sources of wisdom. The energy that flows from this action will allow you to break free from the encumbrances of life and soar even higher.

4.

SIFTING

Listening to Other Voices

Wisdom flows from listening: opening our entire person to the deep truths within us and all around us. We now invite you to listen to the voices of others who lay out various paths to wisdom. As we said earlier, this is a process book, not an effort to defend the merits of a specific path. It makes no difference whether you affirm mindfulness, enjoy communion with nature, identify with the Native American way, listen to chant, walk the way of the body, commune with the goddesses, savor the eternal masculine or feminine, seek a New Age expression to nourish your soul, or follow an obscure and narrow path to the stars as a true believer. The important task is to open your mind and your heart to the riches expressed in a specific way, then glean the wisdom it advocates.

We will select only a few stories, briefly search for their mother lodes of wisdom, then offer some suggestions for reflection. Our intention is to explicate our five processes of growth more clearly. We leave it to you to open up the full implications of a specific path. We also invite you to substitute stories and illustrations of your own as you understand how your individual processes work. Let us begin with an illustration.

"We just moved into our new dream home," she said. "We both worked so hard to get there. The landscaping was done and the place in fine order at last. We sat down to enjoy the surroundings after a hard Saturday of clean-up work. I expected him to follow my lead and talk about how neat it was to be settled in at last. I knew something was bothering him. He was sullen all day long."

Deep disappointment registered in her eyes as she continued. "He informed me that he was tired of the rat race, and that he didn't know whether he wanted to continue doing the hard work related to maintaining a home. I just sat there in stunned silence, doing my best to hear what he said. The more I quieted down, the more he talked.

"Finally, he announced that he planned to move out. He told me he had already signed a lease for an apartment and would be filing for divorce within several days. I thought I was dreaming. When the divorce papers arrived four days later, I knew it was no dream.

"I didn't have much resiliency left after that," she confessed. "I think it must have been eaten up with anger about having to start all over again at the time in our lives when we were finally getting ahead. The rest is kind of a blur to me, but I do remember sitting in the warm sun one glorious autumn morning, looking out over the rolling woodlands where we built this house. The sun warmed and soothed my face and my body, so I simply breathed in its strength. I realized that everything in my life was changing again. I began meditating on the transient nature of all of life. I knew this would be the last morning I would sit in this space. Our dream home would be owned by someone else. The sun continued to energize me. I breathed in more of its warmth and soothing strength, then I just let go. I knew I was ready to move on. I felt free."

This simple example of a "way," associated with the healing energy of the sun, invited this woman to find peace within herself. She is still not sure how it healed her. Perhaps it brought her into solidarity with generations of others who looked toward the sun for revitalization. Perhaps the experience reflects that all life on earth is dependent upon the sun. It might have energized the deep intuitive spirit within her, telling her it is now best to move on.

Even though she cannot clearly identify what happened to her, the experience opened her pathway to rediscovery. The warmth and symbolic meaning of the sunlight filled up the emptiness within her. It supported her direction. In contemporary language, some refer to this as the recovery of soul. Phil Cousineau reflects on the recovery process in this fashion:

> If it's lost, the question becomes, how do you get it back? There is no one path. One way I think we spontaneously try to retrieve our souls is by being around soulful people. Another way is by going to soulful places, either in nature or by way of a pilgrimage to places like Chartres Cathedral or the Wailing Wall of Jerusalem, or even Yankee Stadium. Find those places that are charged with the sacred—places in the world that are holy to us.[6]

Holy places in the world are innumerable, and these places literally echo with the voices of wisdom. The process of sifting implies nothing more than visiting a holy place and listening. We invite you to visit a few of these places with us and listen for the voices that heal.

The Way of Recovered Roots

"I was devastated when he left me," she said. "I actually believed I had found the perfect love and he would always be there to take care of me. I discovered how wrong I was when he announced that he was going to end the relationship. Of course, I was devastated. My fantasies about never feeling lonely again came crashing down around me, then he was gone. We never saw each other again.

"One day," she continued, "while strolling through the downtown area during my lunch break, I walked into the cathedral church where the noonday liturgy is celebrated. I slipped into the back of the church, letting the soft blue light of the stained glass windows shelter me. I relaxed, but was unable to pray. So I simply sat there, trying to absorb everything going on around me. I felt very much at home. My roots are Catholic, but I had been away from anything 'churchy' for ten years. Anyway, I watched people do nothing but pray for an hour, then I finally made a clumsy effort at it myself. Nothing great happened, but I began to feel a kind of a realignment going on inside of me. I sat there after everyone left, stayed very quiet, and knew I needed to open up this part of my life once again."

The recovery of lost roots has the flavor of a homecoming about it. Immersed in the familiar symbols of a less complicated childhood, sifting flows naturally: "What have I missed? What have I thrown away that has caused such emptiness? What do I need to recover? Why did I let him talk me out of such a deep part of my life? What mysterious call do I feel once again that won't let go of me? What has brought me back to this place? How can I put my life in order once again?"

Like the woman in this story, an awakening begins with an experience that life has come full circle. The recovery of deep roots is an invitation to journey once again into a spirituality. It evolves as original gifts are reclaimed, explored, and affirmed.

ǁ Listening to the Song of the Earth ǁ

It is Sedona, Arizona, in early autumn. We look across the open spaces of this holy place, high on the side of Bell Rock. It rests conspicuously on the outskirts of the community, its rounded dome towering a thousand feet above thick pine forests. We rest on a sandstone outcropping of high energy, surrounded in every quadrant by grey and red mountains. We lounge in the warmth of the morning sun, tracing the changing colors of the rocks on the far horizon. Shafts of sunlight stretch across the open spaces below.

Sedona carries an international reputation as an active energy center, calling pilgrims to her from every place on the globe. These people believe that the earth's lines of electromagnetic energy converge there, organizing this high country mecca into a grid, charged to the core for an authentic spiritual quest. Pilgrims acclaim the holiness of the place, giving testimony to its ability to realign their internal landscape with the earth's magnetic field.

For us this day, the expansive panorama all around us surges with positive energy. Every piece of red stone, in every direction we survey, comes alive as a magnificent expression of mighty and mysterious forces that invite our spirits to soar with the falcons riding the warm thermals. We breathe in the fresh pine scent and allow it to become part of us. We listen to the song of the earth and invite it to soothe, support, and captivate us. We experience the personal renewal we often hear people describe as an encounter with Mother Earth.

A gentle kind of sifting takes place, facilitated by forces that flow from the deep connections between body, energy, and creation. It is expansive, often opening out into an awareness that the entire universe shares a consciousness with the human race. It is as close as the next experience of listening.

A walk on the seashore in the early morning, breathing in the sharpness of the salt air while the surf breaks at our feet, reminds us of our brief life compared to the ageless sea. The crunch of autumn leaves under our feet speaks of transitions. A snow day invites us to close in to our holy space and listen to the snowflakes fall. They sing of the close connection between solitude and the discovery of soul.

Wisdom embraces like the softly drifting snow, but it is too soon ignored under the press of commerce or the busyness of life. Wiser voices remind us of the need for solitude. Lynn Andrews suggests the importance of taking the time to discover our basic connection with the earth:

> As individuals and as a society, we must dig deep enough to once again touch the rich earth beneath—deep enough to find the manifestations of nature within our own souls. To do that, it is imperative to find our way into natural settings, into the wilderness. It's there that the soul is healed. It's there that we begin to unite body and soul.[7]

| Listening to the Voice of the Native Americans |

Not so long ago, we took a break from the midwestern winter to absorb a week of warm February sun. The day opened clear and bright, and by late morning we found ourselves at an arts festival at a shopping mall in north Tucson. We listened to classical guitar music while playing under the medicinal sun, like children on early summer vacation.

The vivid reds and blacks of a hand-lettered poster announce that Native American dancers will perform at noon under the atrium of the giant mall. The poster's innocent expressiveness pulls us into the building.

We seat ourselves on steel bleachers among several hundred spectators, and the atrium soon echoes with the thrumming of drums and the high wail of Native American chant. The unusual sounds attract an expanding circle of curious onlookers. They casually scatter themselves around the fringes of the atrium, creating an abrasive din of noise, random motion, and the unnerving congestion associated with active consumerism.

Even so, the Native Americans perform their arts courageously. The first wave of dancers conclude the friendship dance, then sit down, politely acknowledging the crowd's applause.

The atrium belongs for the moment to a young Native American woman. Penetrating dark eyes, accented by a white deerskin dress, define a strong presence in the midst of the confusion and noise. She notes that her flute solo will be a lament for her departed ancestors. "The music is not written down," she confesses. "It is written in my heart. My ancestors believe it is a song that only the heart can record."

The sound system carries the soft melody to the far corners of the atrium. The immediate crowd grows quiet and respectful, while the din of noise and disarray drifts in from the long caverns of the mall.

She finishes her solo, then gives the microphone to her older brother. He begins with a brief story about his long struggle with alcohol and drugs. He notes that he is now released from a treatment facility, where he spent the last several months.

He acknowledges his helplessness in the face of this struggle, and confesses that he found healing only in a return to the sacred traditions of his people. "The most sacred," he announces in a swelling voice, "is the eagle dance. As long as I am able to dance the eagle dance, I will do it not only for my own healing but for all those who long to have their spirits carried before the face of the Great Father. This dance will be dedicated to anyone of you out there who need it."

A few people in the crowd stir slightly. Some look blankly into open space, while their spouses quickly glance their way. The rhythmic thump-thump-thumping of the drums, the hey-yi-yi, hey-yii-yi of ancient chant, aggressively drown out the background noise. The dancer comes to life. His eagle costume lightly etches his spirit into the undefined space as he mimics the flight of the majestic bird. The entire atrium is delivered into the realm of the sacred. Mad activity and rapt attention join in a benediction of modern life. For two enriching hours, the Native Americans carry us outsiders into their sacred space and invite us to drink in their heritage. We stand on solid ground and listen.

Although the story describes a significantly energizing experience for us, the question about the rightful place of Native American spirituality in the lives of non-Native Americans remains abrasive and unresolved. Their spiritualities certainly foster a sensitivity for the sacredness of all life. They invite healing by celebrating the spirits who dwell in all creation. Some Native Americans, however, have expressed concern about the cavalier acceptance of some of their rituals to the exclusion of others. Some forthrightly condemn the desecration of their sacred symbols by whites who use them as fashion statements or ornamental items.

We suggest, however, that a sensitive resolution to this problem rests with listening, rather than gross imitation. We are invited by the eagle dancer and his family to let their rituals speak to us about rediscovering our own roots. In accepting their invitation, we discover a common bond among all those who seek healing.

Dhyani Ywahoo, a Cherokee medicine woman, extends a similar invitation to the human race in this fashion:

> In this time many Native American people are speaking again their ancient wisdom. The message is not to say "Become like an Indian" or to convert people to Native American religion. The old people are saying, "Let us join hands, each as we are, to rebuild the sacred circle of the earth. Let us honor the traditions of all our peoples. Let us know that there is one truth, and all our roots have come from that great tree. Like the salmon, let us come out of the ocean of illusion. Let us be winners in the stream and find our way home again so we may generate new seeds of life."[8]

⊩ Listening for the Buddha: Mindfulness ⊪

The art of mindfulness is to open to an acute awareness of the sacredness of all reality. It invites us to explore the holy space within our souls. In our busy society, a life filled with distractions and intensity is accepted as normal. Pressures of the day, demands of a schedule, expectations for performance, desires for success, can completely govern our lives.

The practice of mindfulness radically reorients a person, opening up a way to deep wisdom. The richest reward of mindfulness comes with the discovery of peace that flows from this ancient way.

Rather than describing what mindfulness is, we invite you to enjoy an experience of it, then pursue a more thorough exploration of its benefits at your leisure. Let the following exercise open up for you a taste of wisdom.

∥ A Simple Meditation ∥

Find your own quiet space, then inhabit it silently for a time. Let your imagination go to work. Picture a trail winding its way upward through the forested mountains ahead of you before disappearing into the tall pines and stately aspens higher on the mountain.

Visualize yourself walking alone on that trail. You are in no hurry to climb to the summit. You slowly walk along, breathing in the fresh pine scent and the beauty of the place. You observe the infinite variations in the ways that the trees grow along the trail: some anchored precariously on the rock face of the mountain, others clustered in spectacular arrangements before opening out into the high meadows above.

You feel the warm sunshine soothe your skin, inviting you to be at peace. The temperature is just right: neither too warm nor too cold. Overhead, the white clouds contrast with the deep blues of the endless mountain sky. You can feel the energy flowing in and through your body as you walk along, still leisurely and calm, breathing in the delicious mountain air.

Breathe in the tranquility of the place. Let it speak to you about how good it is to be alive at this moment. If you become distracted, slowly bring your awareness back to the healing power of this holy place and continue to breathe it in. Remind yourself that you need only to *be* for this moment. Not act. Not hurry. Just *be*.

As you slowly wind your way up the trail, note how safe you feel. The mountain is very friendly. It welcomes you home under its strong protection. Notice that the higher you climb, the more clearly you gain a perspective on the world around you. You can see for miles, noting the intricate patterns laid out on the earth below. You can see the connection between one community and another, the subtle variations in the mountains that line the far horizon.

Be aware that a small change of perspective can offer you a different view of what life holds. You can explore the fresh possibilities that lie open in front of you, which trails lead to light and fulfillment.

Now allow your inner voice to speak to you about how wisdom deepens as you climb higher on the mountain. All wisdom is perspective. Climbing to the heights, taking enough time to gain a good perspective, allows you to feel a quality of wisdom that only comes from the experience of living. Let your wisdom become a part of you.

⊩ Listening for a Voice in the Darkness ⫾

Tom and Cindy were both unhappy in their first marriages, but when their divorces became final, they felt condemned to drift forever on the glassy sea of singleness. When they met by chance on a cruise, their internal compasses registered an irresistible magnetism for each other. It didn't take long for them to dream new dreams of a deep love relationship. Within weeks, they referred to themselves as "soul mates."

Romance opened up both of them to trust again, then one by one they let go of their old fears of intimacy. They discussed marriage as confidently as young executives deal with fiscal projections, promising each other they would never repeat the mistakes of the past. They spoke comfortably about bottom lines relating to top lines in their desire to work for an honest marriage.

Three years later they married, surrounded by family and friends. All seemed well and happy as they departed for their honeymoon, but the disillusionment set in in full force for Cindy just two days after their first anniversary. Tom made several arbitrary decisions about his use of leisure time. He met quietly with several old friends whom Cindy never liked, then enjoyed a leisurely lunch with an old girlfriend while attending a sales conference. When Cindy heard the news from another source, she felt betrayed and angry. She accused him of violating their most important pre-marriage agreement: to jointly plan their lives and to never surprise each other.

Cindy's emotions bubbled over the top line as she confronted Tom about his "exaggerated independence and incredible insensitivity." His anger avalanched beneath the bottom line with accusations of her "insecurity," "reactivity," and "control." Their anger festered for several days, then reached a deafening crescendo late one evening. It became apparent to both of them that the cracks in the edifice of their marriage were deep and unpatchable.

Fresh revelations poured out under the press of serious conflict, and the cracks widened into fissures. Stubborn old patterns of mistrust, hurt, and disappointment resurfaced again and again. When their emotions ebbed long enough to allow each of them to sift, they asked themselves some hard questions: Had they made the wrong decision about getting married? Had they been deceived by their feelings? Should they stay married and find a formula to make it work, or should they divorce each other and set sail again on the solitary sea of a single life?

Their sifting ended in confusion. Neither could decide what he or she wanted. During their stormiest interludes, they were still haunted by their favorite expression, "soul mates." It spoke to them yet about a deep connection of some kind that remained alive even during the storms. A haunting small voice within each of them began to open up the possibility of another approach to their marriage.

Notions of a spirituality were somewhat familiar. Cindy was born and baptized a Catholic, but she remained tentative about her relationship with formal religion. Tom was born a Methodist, but found his hunger for spirituality satisfied through a few New Age forms of expression. It was only when they were confronted with their helplessness, anger, and emptiness, that they began to look more deeply into their own Christian backgrounds.

Kenosis

All spirituality for the Christian begins with the New Testament. We are called to follow in the footsteps of Jesus, whose death on the cross led to his resurrection. The image of Jesus on the cross, totally devoid of all human support and vulnerable to the demands of love as he experienced it, hold up to us an image of how difficult the demands of love can be. Like Jesus, our efforts to love must somehow reflect the movement from death to resurrection.

The Greek term St. Paul used to describe this central invitation to identify with the death and rising of Jesus is *kenosis*. Paul invites us to "think of ourselves the way

Christ Jesus thought of himself." In this classic text, which was actually sung by the early Christians as a hymn, he specifically describes what he means by this invitation:

> He had equal status with God
> but didn't think so much of himself
> that he had to cling to the advantages of that
>   status
> no matter what.
> Not at all.
> When the time came, he set aside the privilege of
>   deity
> and took on the status of a slave, became human!
> Having become human, he stayed human.
> It was an incredibly humbling process.
> He didn't claim special privileges.
> Instead, he lived a selfless, obedient death—
> and the worst kind of death at that: a crucifixion.
> Because of that obedience, God lifted him high
> and honored him far beyond anyone or
>   anything, ever,
> so that all created beings in heaven and on
>   earth—
> even those long ago dead and buried—
> will bow in worship before this Jesus Christ,
> and call out in praise that he is the master of all,
> to the glorious honor of God the Father.
>
> (Philippians 2: 5–11)

This simple hymn beautifully summarizes the most traditional of all the Christian traditions. To accept this invitation is to stand in a holy place. It is a light that beckons to us in the darkness, a clear voice that calls out to us from the noise of life. In marriage, it is an invitation to examine and purify love, in order to encounter the God who dwells in the unexplored strata of the relationship.

‖ Kenosis in a Marriage ‖

When a marriage changes, even though the changes represent deep and sometimes unnerving developmental processes, a couple is not by that fact immersed in the dynamic of kenosis. Rather than bringing a rich spiritual renewal, the changes for some bring unrelenting emptiness, or even an end to the marriage. The tenuous search for self-fulfillment, the difficulties of understanding what is going on within the relationship itself, denial, evasion, and unbridled emotions can severely alienate a husband and wife from each other as well as from God.

But if a couple honestly searches for a spirituality, the process of change can offer abundant material for an opportunity to think of themselves in the same way that Jesus thinks of himself. It is in this identification that God is invited into the marriage to heal, to transform, and to be an unseen partner in the development of mature love.

In brief, God is present within all realities, every process of change. When life collapses, the Christian view invites us to listen for that voice that encourages us to look more deeply and live more authentically. We invite God to reconstruct with us. The continued story of Tom and Cindy can shed some light on what we mean.

After weeks of deepening encounters, they began to realize that their desire for happiness seduced them to jointly construct a fantasy of the perfect love. Their talk of bottom lines and top lines was nothing more than a stylized effort to protect themselves from future hurt. The collapse of their fantasy brought with it plenty of empty feelings, but feelings alone did not signal a time of genuine kenosis. That transition came later.

They talked at length about divorce, but they determined that the expression "soul mates" still touched them deeply enough to sift for life within the deeper potential for the marriage. They took the first tentative steps that St. Paul describes as "taking on the mind of Christ." In brief, they began to turn their thoughts toward a marriage more open to a lived spirituality. They admitted that if God is to become a part of their marriage, they must make more room for God in their hearts.

By prayerfully listening to what their own emptying-out was telling them, they began to let go of their unrealistic expectations for each other. Prayer began to fill some of the emptiness created by unfulfilled expectations. They forgave each other. They began to understand that married love can be reflective of the unconditional love of God, even for them.

Kenosis brought with it a different way to empty out their stubbornness, denial, anger, and fantasies of undisturbed, placid love. They slowly understood that it is God who transforms weaknesses into real strength, fears into confidence, and self-serving into genuine love. This conversion of heart led to the opening up of a genuine wisdom.

Two years after the grounding experience of their long nights of truth, Tom and Cindy still have their doubts. Their life is far from perfect, but they continue to grow. They know that if the dark forces at work within each of them are allowed to run unchecked, they can still be outrageously blaming and vindictive. They also discovered that when they slip back into their old patterns of entanglement, they are now able to pray more honestly. Prayer now involves the surrender of their pettiness, stubbornness, and childhood dreams of the perfect love. They work hard to hear each other more clearly. They ask God to help them heal whatever parts of their relationship remain messy and stubborn.

They still hold on to their desires to have a good marriage, but their notions of what constitutes a good one have matured. They still call one another "soul mates," but the phrase now carries an entirely different meaning. They have a clearer understanding that the God of love speaks to them through their continued development. Their experiences confirm for them what some of the great spiritual writers have noted: we learn more about God from surrender than by abstract reasoning. Deep transformation is more a matter of the heart than the intellect.

They realize that their unbalancing experiences have taught them something about looking for wisdom. Their lives are an embodiment of what the Scriptures suggest about looking for its presence:

> Wisdom is bright, and does not grow dim.
> By those who love her she is readily seen,
> and found by those who look for her.
> Quick to anticipate those who desire her,
> she makes herself known to them.
>
> (Wisdom 6:12)

| Listening to the Wisdom of the Body |

"With the onset of midlife and the loss of my mother at the same time," she said, "the focus for my life was just fragmented. She was my last parent. I had neither the strength nor the desire to continue. It took hard effort just to get my daily work done. I had no energy left to extend myself to new activities, so I vegged out and gained thirty-five pounds. Then I really felt bad."

Stories like this are as common as the reality of deep losses in life. The sadness is often translated into a blockage of energy; hence, creativity ceases. We observe that this state of lethargy overrides even the desire for good health. Consequently, the neglect of some basic health habits compounds the emptiness. A chronic state of negative energy exists.

Yet a simple sifting through body-focused options for regaining positive energy points to the value of creating and maintaining good health habits: a balanced diet, plenty of rest, and regular exercise. We also live in an era when the human community enjoys a virtual blossoming of paths to free up positive bodily energy: massage therapies of various kinds, acupressure techniques, aerobic and anaerobic exercise routines, health food modalities, therapeutic touch, and various types of body work. The list of possibilities is far too long to describe in detail. We leave the specific exploration of these paths for you, and simply affirm the relative merits of each of them. As in any journey leading to engendered wisdom, its depth flows from how well you walk the path.

We simply suggest that the body contains within it an abundance of wisdom, and it can be tapped and channelled into a new creativity through the use of these techniques. Blockages that seriously impede the flow of creativity can be directly assessed, then opened up through some of the techniques. The body is envisioned as an energy grid, operating with some of the same principles that govern the flow of energy in any complex reality. With the right manipulation, the correct focus, or an effort to free blocked passageways, energy begins to flow again. Creativity returns. Life rights itself. The body comes to life and resonates with a wisdom that is deeply experienced.

We usually recommend a program of routine and consistent exercise, not only during times of change, but as part of a regular daily schedule. The body has a wonderful capacity to rejuvenate itself, and we usually find that as the body heals, so does the spirit.

"I got sick and tired of feeling so depleted and looking so unattractive," she continued. "I joined a program at a diet center, bought a membership in a health club, hired a fitness consultant to help me get my self-esteem back. They all remind me of my commitment to be healthy again, and six months later there is twenty-five pounds less of me. I'm feeling much better and plan to continue down this track of getting fit once again."

This connection between a balance of the body and the balance of the mind is described by Joseph Goldstein and Jack Kornfield:

> At certain deep stages sitting meditation itself can bring energy and lightness to the body. But most practitioners find that this is not sufficient. Through mindful yoga, stretching, regular aerobic exercise, and movement we can help make the body a more supple vehicle for the powerful energy practice to open within us. As practice develops we must nourish mindfulness by learning to care for our bodies and live more fully in the present.[9]

⫼ A Meditation on the Body: Breathing ⫼

As in any body-focused effort to regain energy, the simple exercise of reflective breathing can be healing. This

simple approach to meditation is often used as an intro-
duction to other forms of mindfulness. Some speak of the
practice as a form of centering.

One man describes its personal benefits in this fashion: "I start my day this way and it is essential for me. The
simple practice of finding quiet space, focusing on my
breathing, then rediscovering my own center has sustained
me through some very big changes in my life. The practice
of deep breathing brings me into alignment with my roots.
I know that breath is the connection between my real self
and my Creator. I sometimes move into deep prayer,
knowing that I am enlivened with the breath of God."

We suggest this simple exercise of breathing to give
you an idea of what we mean:

1. Find a quiet place somewhere, in a private space in
   which you are free of distractions. If it is marginal, take
   charge of your surroundings: get rid of the phone for a
   time or make a request to your family that you be left
   alone. Make sure you have twenty minutes to be free to
   explore your inner space.
2. Seat yourself in a comfortable, yet erect, posture. Begin
   your exercise by concentrating on your breath. Inhale
   through your nose and exhale through your mouth.
   Allow your breathing to slow down as you get underway.
3. Concentrate on the process of breathing itself. Note how
   you feel as your lungs bring in fresh oxygen. Relax a little
   more each time you exhale. Give permission to your
   body to slow down as you become more aware of your
   rhythmic breathing.
4. Use a sacred word, repeating it slowly to yourself as
   your breathing deepens. A simple word like "calm" or
   "peace" will be fine. The use of a word like this helps you
   focus on staying centered. Some imagine that their

breathing is an expression of creative energy flowing into them from their Creator. You can repeat a simple word as a mantra, like "ABBA" (Father) or "AMMA" (Mother). This simple repetition often opens up the mind into a quiet form of prayer, in relationship to the Father-God or Mother-God.

5. Remain in your relaxed position for twenty minutes, allowing new energy to flow into your body. Give yourself permission to feel your body coming to life. Savor it. Feel good about it. Be aware that the energy is offering you a foundation that carries over into every dimension of your life. It touches mind, heart, and soul.

6. Let your body clock tell you when twenty minutes have elapsed. Slowly reorient yourself to waking life. Enjoy the feeling of being centered. Feel yourself gathering up new energy as you prepare for another day. Think of yourself as now energized and ready to begin the routine of living, marked by an excitement about being alive.

Sifting for a Balance: Inward and Outward Energy

As we have suggested previously, sifting for the sources of wisdom takes a variety of forms. As the wisdom gleaned from a specific path becomes integrated into the practicality of living, it becomes increasingly more difficult to define a clear boundary between the voices from within and the voices from without. That matters little, however, for both the inward and the outward sources bring with them their own validity and manifest their own beauty.

We encourage you to listen to the voice that speaks to you most clearly about wisdom, energy, clarity, and hope. The voices come clearly to some, so the clarity carries with it an aura of a genuine gift from above. For others, the efforts to listen, the long-term sifting, and the struggle to find a genuine self, create great strain. The drama to find life takes place within an emotional state that is painful and empty. Some listen for years, straining to hear any voice that will rescue them from their deep self-doubts. When they finally hear a voice that refreshes them, they hold it to their breast and proclaim it as a great prize. It becomes a part of them.

5.

RECONSTRUCTION

Out of the Ashes, a New Self

Change is the one constant in life, pushing the individual to search for continuity within a stream of alteration and flux. When the sifting process runs its course, the desire to reconstruct comes easily, bringing with it a fresh definition of what constitutes reality. The future begins to take shape around a predictable form. A new self evolves.

Life begins again. People shift gears, whether it is a labored reaction to downsizing or the willful embrace of a simpler life. Couples decide to love one another, even if their spouse is less than perfect. Others go their separate ways. Individuals make new friends. Career changes mark the mid-life quest. Some go back to college, proclaiming that it is now their turn for an education. The reconstruction process gives form to their dreams. Wisdom is integrated and fresh energy released.

In the final analysis, all the sifting for wisdom, all the efforts at growth, all the descriptive language of spirit and soul, evolve into an internalized composite of personal gain we refer to as the true self. It begins to take charge more and more.

The true self becomes the ground for the deepest stability within the person. It speaks with the voice of intuition, directing life with astuteness and care. It bows before the face of external wisdom, ever open to growth. Thus, it forms a continuity from one day to the next, applying the great lessons of life with creativity and confidence.

Even though the true self forms the bedrock of stability, creativity, and continuity as our five processes unfold toward maturity, it remains a difficult entity to describe and understand. In an effort to establish a solid and credible basis for the five processes, we will explore the central function of the self at some depth. Allow us to begin with another story.

The Story of An Evolving Self

"Osteoporosis," she said, slowly shaking her head back and forth in disbelief. "It's certain, now. My doctor told me this morning that I have osteoporosis."

We remain silent as we absorb the news. She sat rigidly upright, her lower back supported by a small pillow, since the framework of her body continued to weaken. She now understood the origin of her stiffness, chronic aches, and arthritic pain.

"The doctors tell me that I have already lost 30 percent of my calcium and I must move carefully," she said quietly. "I'm already at the bone-breaking stage."

We face her squarely, letting the hard news sink into our collective bones. In the quiet pauses, she cries softly. "My clinic sent along this brochure," she continued, "written for victims of osteoporosis. Want to hear what they recommend?"

"Sure," we answer.

"It says that I need to be positive, do gentle exercise—

being careful not to break any bones—and develop a new self-image. That's all," she laughed with a shrug. Then we all laugh aloud, nodding our heads in unison at the understatement.

Our discussion takes flesh around a long litany of traumatic incidents, including the loss of her first husband to cancer. Although the divorce was finalized prior to his illness, she returned to his bedside for long night vigils. A second marriage invited new difficulties, but she somehow found the energy to deal with it. She explored her life openly, our shared efforts slowly taking substance around her development of a more authentic self.

The word *self* appears often in the literature of growth and development, and it generally describes a deep center for thoughts, feelings, and attitudes. Like any complex structure that begins as disparate pieces before solidifying into a solid substance, the self is usually imaged as becoming more whole through the growth experience. As it becomes more integrated, it is described as an authentic self, a whole self, a true self, a real self, even a higher self. Each term sheds light on its dynamic quality as well as its open-endedness. We prefer to use the phrase *the true self.* As the self becomes more integrated, it is imagined as a metaphorical base camp for a climb to the summit of good functioning. Some see the true self as the seat of wisdom and source of intuition.

The self functions like an internal guidance system. It is a primary sifting site as the search for wisdom opens up. The self is the solid space within that asks the questions, sorts the options, then measures the merits of new approaches to life. It suggests practical ways to synthesize that wisdom into a core of beliefs, feelings, and attitudes that offer the person direction and energy. When the familiar structures of life collapse, including our bodies, the self remains. When the fantasies that undergird major change collapse, a true self sustains the person.

Psychological realities can be vague, and the self is no exception. Consequently, defining the self can be a complex and frustrating task. There is no universally accepted definition. For the sake of constructing a thoughtful foundation for this stage of our process, we offer the following definition:

> The real self, from the perspective of object relations theory, is made up of the sum of the intrapsychic images of the self and of significant others, as well as the feelings associated with those images, along with the capacity for action in the environment guided by those images.[10]

Rather than laboring over an academic discussion of the existence and the components of the self, we prefer to examine it from a practical point of view. In doing so, we can apply the notion of the true self to our reflections on process more easily.

We note, in our daily work with people, that as they move from a life encumbered with fantasy to a reflective maturity, they change with the process. Something discernible firms up deep within them, anchoring them into a more positive relationship with themselves, their significant others, and their environment. This, we contend, is the developing self. When they trust it, allow it to govern their lives more directly, and then move them toward a life overseen by an active intuition, we speak of the emergence of the true self.

Like an internal guidance system that tracks a giant aircraft across large expanses of the open sea, the true self guides a person through the ambiguity of life. They find direction during times of change. They depend less upon the direction of others. They listen more trustingly to their inner voice. Ultimately, the true self leads the person through the process of change, points them toward maturity, and offers the foundation for a dynamic spirituality. Self-possession and confidence are evident in all that they are.

| Characteristics of the New Self |

We now wish to describe several of the important qualities of the new self, then reflect on their relevance for a deepening wisdom. These qualities become building blocks in the reconstruction process, genuinely integrating into a whole as the person matures. In trying to describe the unique mix of these qualities for the individual person, we rely as much on stories and illustrations as on abstract language.

| Self-Direction |

Tom's mother died one year after his father, and he found himself alone and adrift. He felt the full sting of his orphanhood like no other pain in his life.

He turned his energies to settling his mother's estate, and was midway through his task when he slipped into a dark depression. Tom believed his sadness would lift if he just kept busy, but it stubbornly refused to do so. Nothing gave him relief.

His desperation to find relief brought him to professional help. There he confirmed that his wrenching sadness related to his losses, but the darkness still refused to lift. Under the gentle coaching of his therapist, Tom finally admitted to himself that he carries a great deal of anger at his parents.

At first, he felt guilty about his anger, but the more he talked, the more he discovered the stubborn depths of his dilemma. He wanted to be free of parental control, but he couldn't break out of his imagined loyalty to them. This entrapment remained even though they were both dead. He felt especially bad about missing an opportunity for marriage when he was thirty years old, choosing instead to take care of his parents in their old age.

As he came to more honest terms with his life, he discovered that his fears of independence were far more debilitating than the demands of his parents. He finally admitted that he placed too much blame on them for his emptiness. As he understood the full complexity of his emotions, he learned to talk about them without guilt. To his surprise, his depression began to lift. He felt free for the first time in his life. He also felt relieved that he no longer needed to shut down his life in order to please his parents. He now feels emotions he never felt before and he is learning to enjoy them. He even took some of his inheritance money and bought a sports car, in complete contrast to his typically conservative lifestyle.

Now free of the emotional constrictions that governed most of his life, Tom is learning to redirect his life in a way that is significant to him, rather than to others. As his mourning lessens, he is becoming more sure of his newly-formed self. Even though he still misses his parents, he now takes great pleasure in directing his life the way he desires. The redirection is observable to everyone who knows him.

‖ Spontaneity ‖

As our five processes evolve from an early state of disintegration to a mature self, the person experiences life in a richer and more rewarding mode. The capacity to laugh at one's self comes to life. A richer emotional life evolves. Some feelings are new; others return, although once believed dead. The person discovers a pleasant interpersonal spinoff from their hard work: their friends enjoy being around them once again. Some develop new friends, in contrast to their previous isolation. Life opens up into a fresh expression of creativity and that brings with it renewed vitality. Like the full spectrum of color in a rainbow, their emotions begin to reflect deep hues and rich colors. We describe all of these shifts as spontaneity.

‖ Self-Esteem ‖

As the real self emerges from the ashes of change, it expresses itself in a fresh appreciation of one's own person. We refer to this as a renewal of self-esteem. A peacefulness evolves. The person feels good about him-or herself. The good feelings become apparent during times of solitude as well as during interaction with significant others.

"I discovered through my own isolation," she confessed, "that I had done some awful things to my friends. I really believed that I deserved very little in life, so I became adept at pushing people away. Then I blamed them for never paying enough attention to me."

Her moment of discovery evolved at a time when the one relationship she really valued collapsed. She laid it to final rest through the increasing demands that evacuated it of every ounce of expressiveness and spontaneity. Her friend's farewell statement came in the same announcement that she was choking him to death.

The loss of this love devastated her. Its collapse drove her into the deepest reevaluation of her life. There she examined the themes of isolation that drove her life, then made a decision that she would no longer be enslaved by them. That decision allowed her to feel more positive about herself, and she began to place more emphasis upon developing her good qualities.

As difficult as this was at first, she followed through with her resolutions. The shift in priorities began to change the texture of her relationships. She became less dependent upon them. She discovered she no longer needed them for emotional survival. Consequently, she no longer pushed her friends to the limits of their patience by constantly testing their loyalty.

"I have learned," she said, "that I can feel good about myself through some very simple activities: gardening, creative decorating in my home, and a variety of other actions that are important to me. I have lightened up on myself. It feels right for me. The nice part about all of this is that I have actually cultivated a few close friends. They genuinely care for me and I for them. I have learned to cultivate these relationships as carefully as I do my flowers." The riches of a solid self-esteem now belong to her.

ǁ The Enjoyment of Solitude ǁ

"I find myself seeking more solitude," she stated. "I love it. I used to run away from quiet time but now find that I seek it in order to refresh myself. It wasn't too long ago that I needed people around me all the time. I still have a lot of good friends but my alone time is just as important as constant interaction.

"I now live with much more of a balance," she continued. "I am not so vulnerable to what others are thinking or so sensitive about how they relate to me. A couple of my old friends really got angry at me because I speak about myself in ways they can't handle. A year ago, I would have retracted my statements with an apology for being so insensitive. No more."

Her candid description seemed heartfelt and honest. She remains strong and unapologetic in her confession about the discovery of a new center for her life. It is intimately tied to her capacity to take time out and center herself through regular meditation. There she discovers the joy of being grounded in a self that she trusts. She knows intuitively that her life is more real.

As we so often see in our work, the desire to seek quiet time, enjoy its beauty, and learn to find a deep wisdom within, are all marks of a maturing self.

Susan L. Taylor speaks in this way about the connection between solitude and wisdom:

> The wisdom and strength you seek awaits you in the silence within. Awakening to our deepest desires, to our needs and to our truth requires reflection and inner listening. We must create the space in our lives where our physical self and our spiritual being can meet.[11]

‖ Seeking a Meaningful Intimacy ‖

The enjoyment of a genuine intimacy is just as important as the enjoyment of solitude, but sometimes in the aftermath of change, this presents a challenge.

Tom and Shelly had just celebrated their twenty-third wedding anniversary when they sought marital therapy. Their last child was now safely boarded at a state university, opening up the space for the two of them to enjoy cruises, golf outings, and a more leisurely approach to life.

Their first year alone, however, brought with it an unexpected turn of events: they found themselves fighting constantly. Each exchange ended with frustration and bitterness about their inability to problem-solve, after so many years of being successful at it. They would remain distant and resentful for several days after a fight. Efforts to forgive and forget lasted for a brief period of time before the clashes began again.

After much joint soul-searching in marital therapy, they began to understand that simple matters of closeness were more demanding than they anticipated.

They discovered that they were encumbered by long-term reservations about closeness, but these reservations were masked during the long years of child-rearing. As long as they remained busy with the demands of parenting, they could side-step unspoken hesitancies about intimacy. Fighting now insulated them from confronting the difficult questions about their capacity to handle intimacy.

Once they began to understand the connection between fighting and their uncertainty about closeness, they reignited an excitement about their marriage. They supported each other to chart a course that led to a more authentic self for each, one that was more at home with the independence associated with the middle years. This maturing also helped them accept the real differences in their persons.

They then learned to express their reservations about closeness more candidly, rather than setting up conflict as an indirect way to create distance. They became more honest about their real needs. Their marriage healed dramatically in six months, and they rewarded themselves for their good work with a lengthy trip to Ireland.

ǁ Creativity ǁ

As the true self develops, it frees up previously trapped, misdirected, or misused energy. This facilitates a creative reconstruction, inwardly and outwardly.

"I worried so much about doing things correctly," she confessed. "I always second-guessed myself. I tried so hard to please others that I never really had the time to please myself."

This young woman's dilemma is clear. She spent most of her life seeking approval from others. She would frequently become immobilized, waiting cautiously for a signal from someone in authority to give her permission to act.

This cautiously constructed approach to life sustained her until age thirty-five, then she fell into a deep depression. It refused to lift. Medication allowed her to function, but she still lacked a life free of her crippling fears of failure and disappointment.

After months of hard work, a breakthrough came one afternoon when she exclaimed, "I am so sick and tired of having everyone else run my life." The emotional intensity behind this declaration even caught her by surprise.

Her therapist followed her lead then, over the next few months, helped her explore the complex network of entrapments, obligations, guilt, and uncertainty that constricted her life. As she became more aware of how completely her fears entrapped her, she began to feel a new self evolving deep within her. She also admitted that she liked it.

"I finally made some decisions for myself," she confessed one day, "and I like what I feel. The freedom is wonderful. Now, instead of spending all my energy worrying about what other people are thinking, I put it into creating new life."

┆ Continuity ┆

"It has taken me a long time to get there, but I have finally made some decisions about who I am and what I want," he declared. His statement came after a long period of sifting and reconstructing.

He suffered through the failure of one marriage and remains immersed in the hard work of making a second one work. He survived one downsizing of his company. Now the next one threatens to disrupt the order of life at any time. Worries about job security dominate his awareness like a dark cloud of oppression.

"I finally arrived at a simple conclusion one afternoon," he said. "Rumors were flying all over the office once again about the company relocating in another state. Every person I talked with was on the edge of a panic attack. I stay angry about the situation like them, but I decided I am tired of feeling angry. It saps all my energy. In a moment of clarity, it just sort of came to me that no one is going to make my life work except me, and that became a turning point."

His manner calmed as he described his new awareness. "I moved toward a more determined course of action," he said. "Even though I don't know what to expect from the future, I figure I've made my life work for the last fifty years, so I can sure as hell make it work for whatever years are left. Every time I repeat that to myself, I feel free."

The true self moves the person through the fluidity of day-to-day life, but with continuity. Like this man, if you trust that it will lead you through life in a productive fashion, it will.

It matters little whether the task is fostering intimacy, assuming a leadership role, dealing with conflict, or creating something of benefit for the coming generations. The true self anchors a person in reality, and orients them toward a life that is open, honest, and caring. The true self governs, directs, and grounds a person in a consistent and satisfying approach to life. It leads to a peacefulness and self-possession.

This is how James Masterson, M.D., describes the connection between the real self and day-to-day continuity:

> The real self has a sense of continuity; it creates a tough core at the center of one's identity that remains the same from one experience or crisis to another.[12]

‖ Compassion ‖

The true self operates with compassionate sensitivity. It extends outwardly to others as well as inwardly toward one's own goodness. Compassion thereby becomes the most tender and expansive of all the qualities of the self. This reconstruction is an especially important one, because compassion bridges time and eternity. It underlies an expansiveness that carries a person outside the limited confines of life and into an awareness of the unity of all reality. It can identify with a higher consciousness. It leads to an encounter with God, since an encounter with the compassionate God comes through a meeting of compassionate hearts.

Jacquelin Small speaks of compassion's deep connections with the universe in this way:

> As we develop this for ourselves, it begins spilling out to others. We love and see others as we love and see ourselves. Compassion is feeling, but it is not ego-involved feeling. It stands on the sidelines and weeps for humankind. Then it moves in and acts, where it can, for others. It draws diversity back into itself, realizing the unity behind everything.[13]

In summary, we see the true self as the most grounded and grounding of all the sources of success in life. It also opens to mystery. It is that still point within that observes the heavens in awe, or hosts an encounter with a personal God.

Sam Keen explores the deep connection between spirit and self, but then resolves his questions in an admission of mystery:

> The first glimmerings of awareness that the self is spirit may come in the experience of discovering a silent and untroubled point within the chaos of the personality....I overflow my personality. Who am I? What is my ultimate identity? What are the ultimate boundaries of this being I call myself? I don't know.[14]

6.

REINTEGRATION

The True Self

It is impossible to say when the true self opens toward the transcendent. Stories differ immensely as people move through our five processes of change. Contemporary spiritualities proliferate as well in our time, blurring a hard distinction between the secular and the sacred.

We suggest that any efforts to reflect creatively on life or to start over with a more determined effort to make it work are genuine expressions of transcendence. At the center of reintegration evolves the true self. Its full dimensions remain hidden in mystery or await their finality in an encounter with the living God. To explore what we mean, we return to the story of the woman afflicted with osteoporosis.

"My husband," she reflected, glancing at her hands, "I worry about my husband. Will he continue to love me as this thing progresses? Will he find any compassion for me?

"What is going to happen to me? What about all the work we have done to help me grow? Does it really mean anything? Will it disappear if I should die? I feel like my whole life has been shattered. What's left for me now?"

We sat in silence for a time, waiting for some kind of concrete answer to her hard questions. They evolved slowly, hesitatingly, while we weighed the full implications of what she asked.

"The true self," we suggest, "allows you to transcend even the most significant changes and find continuity for your life."

"Cancer," she continued, unimpressed by our arguments, "invades your system like an alien intruder and you can localize it, but this…," she said, glancing at the back of her hands again. "This is insidious, like your whole internal structure is eroding away."

"Which part will my husband love now?" she asked. "Will he only love the 70 percent of me that is healthy? Or will he also love the part of me that is eroding? Will he be there for me if I become bedfast?"

Osteoporosis is a disease characterized by a severe degradation of bone mass and density. The very framework for the whole body becomes fragile and brittle, making the simplest of tasks dangerous. Spaces between the bones become enlarged, leading to a chronic arthritic condition. The degradation is usually measured in terms of calcium gone (30 percent) and calcium remaining (70 percent).

The origins of the disease are usually secluded by age, post-menopausal changes, genetics, dietary deficiency or trauma. The strength of the skeletal system is clearly tied to gravity and exercise. It is a routine occurrence for astronauts to return to earth with seriously decreased bone mass. Some of the Russian cosmonauts were unable to walk after their long days in a space capsule, and the standard remedy is now to include an on-board exercise program.

The overall impact of osteoporosis, however, can't be measured in percentages of calcium lost or retained. The victim can spend weeks waiting for a broken bone to heal, only to break another upon reentry into active living. The emotional spinoffs are isolation, depression, anxiety, and a continuing deterioration of the quality of life. Questions surface easily about the outcome of life, one's future, even one's mortality. The disease easily becomes metaphorical for hard questions about life and immortality: what is transient and what is permanent? What remains when the body collapses? What is significant and lasting when all appears to be dying around me?

Is there more to the person than the psychological realities? Indeed, is there a deeper self of some sort that remains even when the physical self is deteriorating? Or gone? What do I encounter in the sacred? Is this the space that brings an encounter with a personal God? We suggest that the evolution of the true self touches on all these questions.

Opening up the transcendent dimensions of the true self usually flows from a deep experience of unexplainable magnitude. The experience usually invites the person to expand the known boundaries of the self. We often hear people speak about the self diffused into a cosmic awareness, as if they are cast out among the stars to find a home there. Once this expansive experience is reintegrated into a new awareness of one's place in the universe, change takes on a new face. Transitions are viewed and experienced from a much broader perspective. Continuity becomes grounded in an experience of transcendence. People see reality differently. They know that their destiny is bigger than the simple structures of reality, the dictates of organizational life, or the routine of daily living. Consequently, change comes more easily.

A Change of Perspective

Each person possesses a limited perspective on life, gleaned from their small vantage point in an ever-expanding universe. Consequently, our capacity to deal with change also suffers from a limited perspective, compared to those who enjoy a more privileged vision of what's real. Listen to the voice of the Russian cosmonaut Boris Volynov as he speaks of the expansiveness associated with a space flight:

> During a space flight, the psyche of each astronaut is reshaped. Having seen the sun, the stars, and our planet, you become more full of life, softer. You begin to look at all living things with greater trepidation and you begin to be more kind and patient with the people around you. [15]

Of course, few enjoy the privileged position of a cosmonaut. Perhaps if we were similarly privileged, all change, all reality would be easily seen as a gift flowing from a unified cosmos. Our evolution into a true self would flow with little hesitation.

We can, however, approximate this peaceful evolution by taking the time to listen to the universe as it exists around us. It can be as close as opening our eyes.

"I vividly remember floating down Hell's Canyon of the Snake River that week," he related. "The days were hot and clear, and brought their green beauty. But the nights are something else. Such a spectacle. We camped on the low hills just above the river bank. There are no surrounding lights, so the view of the night sky is spectacular. We were so tired from a day on the river that we usually slept peacefully through till morning. One night—it must have been about three in the morning—I awakened and turned my face sky-ward. The night sky was alive, and the more I looked, the more it opened up to me. It possessed such a rich texture, such depth. It captivated me so much, I felt like it was speaking to me. Satellites slid by, meteors streaked across the dark spaces above me. I stayed awake for three solid hours, taking deep delight in the constantly changing night spectacle. I saw physical beauty I had never seen before. Even more than that, I felt some kind of identification with the universe. It sort of lifted me out of my small position on the bank of the river and brought me into a unity with what I observed. I hardly knew myself as a separate consciousness, only a part of a larger consciousness that saturated me. It put me in a reflective mood that lasted the rest of the trip."

It makes little difference whether we define this experience as the discovery of a cosmic self, the gift of contemplation, the expression of the true self, or a unitive experience. Awareness opened out for this man into a unity with the cosmos. The way that he deals with life changed at that moment, and it still remains active within him. Problems, changes, and transitions of various kinds are still framed as necessary shifts on the surface of his life. His view allows him to deal with them expediently but calmly. He possesses the gift of a genuine transcendence.

Gerald May describes some of the qualities of the unitive experience in a more detached language than that used by the man in the account above. He suggests a sense of homecoming:

> There is something here that has the quality of going home after a long journey. It is as if the unitive world is the place we truly come from, a constant and steadfast source that is wholly

uncluttered by our frenetic doings and preoccu-
pations. [16]

Our task is simply to listen for these experiences, and
we don't need to be a cosmonaut in order to find them.
They are readily available to everyone. The practice of listening as an exercise of meditation can bridge the gap
between our limited perspectives and the invitation of the
true self to open up to transcendence. Julia Cameron, who
has applied the meditative process to the artist's way of
discovery, describes the opening up like this:

> We meditate to discover our own identity, our
> right place in the scheme of the universe.
> Through meditation, we acquire and eventually
> acknowledge our connection to the inner power
> source that has the ability to transform our outer
> world. In other words, meditation gives us not
> only the light of insight but also the power for
> expansive change. [17]

‖ Encounters with God ‖

For Christians, explorations of the true self are intimately connected to an encounter with the living God. In
order to understand this flowering, we turn to the work of
Thomas Merton. His studies on the evolution of the true
self place that reality at the center of all his works. It is an
orienting concept around which he developed a serious
theology of the self. [18]

He systematically explored the question of the deeper
self for most of his life, and his studies led him to form a
bridge between Western and Eastern notions of the self. He
pointed to the development of the true self as the fulfill-

ment of everything human. It is the ground for an encounter with a personal God. Although his language is heavily theological and some of his statements lack the sensitivity of a contemporary vocabulary of inclusiveness, his reflections speak to us about human destiny:

> Ultimately, the only way I can be myself is to become identified with Him in whom is hidden the reason and fulfillment of my existence. Therefore there is only one problem on which all of my existence, my peace and my happiness depend: to discover myself in discovering God. If I find Him I will find myself and if I find my true self I will find Him. [19]

Perspectives on life change with the deep evolution of the true self. The mystery is grounded in God, and as the true self comes to life, old attitudes, old perceptions and images fall away like masks. Thus, the discovery of the true self is really the deep work of transformation hidden in God.

> The "I" that works in the world, thinks about itself, observes its own reactions and talks about itself is not the true "I" that has been united to God in Christ. It is at best the vesture, the mask, the disguise of that mysterious and unknown "self" whom most of us will never discover until we are dead. Our external, superficial self is not eternal, not spiritual. Far from it. This self is doomed to disappear as completely as smoke from a chimney. It is utterly frail and evanescent. [20]

"What about my body?" asks the woman with osteoporosis. "What is to be left of me as this thing progresses? Will my self go with it? I'm really fearful."

"Our view says that as your body changes your person becomes more grounded in God," we say again. "We have no doubts about that. We believe you are called to life through a dying process. We all are," we reassure her, but "some of us just haven't been confronted with the stark facts as dramatically as you have. Therefore, we live undisturbed with our fantasies about how solid life is."

Discovering the true self invites more than just our own labor. For Merton, and others, the true self opens out into the ground of our being, who is God. Therefore, to enter the realm of the sacred is as much God's work as our own. It is God who gives us life; it is God who plants the desire in us to find fulfillment in love. Like Sam Keen, Merton suspends his reflections on the true self in a sense of mystery:

> ...there is no human and rational way in which I
> can arrive at that contact, that possession of Him,
> which will be the discovery of Who He really is
> and Who I am in Him... The only one who can
> teach me to find God is God, Himself, Alone. [21]

‖ Profound Listening ‖

At the center of our view about the riches that evolve through the development of the true self, we discover the God of unconditional love. For those who genuinely desire it, God slowly unfolds a deep insightfulness into the sacredness of all life as God offers an engaging wisdom. As we slowly awaken to God's initiative, God becomes more active in our processes, causing us to soar to heights we cannot reach unaided. We speak of this development as the gift of profound listening. Some call it the gift of contemplation.

God not only gives us the capacity to listen, God fills

our senses with an ever-deepening richness that is God. God not only bestows the ability to hear, God writes beautiful music. God not only bestows the ability to see, God fills the heavens with stars and establishes our oneness with them. God not only invites us to feel compassion, God *is* compassion, and we absorb God through deep knowledge of the heart.

With the flowering of these gifts, the perspective about what life holds changes. A clarity emerges, a purity of soul. What was once important is no longer significant. Values change. Knowing God becomes more important than success in any area of life.

The process of sifting continues, slowly separating what is of greater value from the lesser. An evolution takes shape over time. Life becomes cleaner and more purified. Change is of lesser consequence because God's love transcends every other reality, textures every interpretation of the significance of change.

"The two of you sound so convincing," smiles the woman with osteoporosis. "I'm not too sure about everything you say. I don't know how to open up my life that easily. I'm having enough trouble just keeping myself together. I am beginning to trust more. I certainly want to trust myself and, hopefully, God. My views are clearing, and I have learned to pray again." We listen and say nothing.

The foundation for living well, seeking a richer connection with others, then moving toward a deep union with God, resides within the mystery of the true self. The natural expression of this deep wisdom is to learn to trust: to trust the self, to trust the universe, to trust our intuition.

7.

TRANSCENDENCE

Trusting the Voice Within

As the path to wisdom approaches the summit of the mountain, it claims a voice of its own. We call this the voice of intuition. To listen to it is to honor the true self. Sifting is behind for a time; life is reconstructing, while the voice points the way to the summit. The true self begins to know what is best for us, and there is little left to do but give it permission to lead. Again, allow us to illustrate.

"I should have listened to myself," she cried. "I let someone talk me into being something other than I am and now I have to face the consequences."

Deeply saddened by the turn of events in her life, she began exploring the aftershocks of a collapsed relationship. On the eve of treatment, she terminated a two year relationship with the significant male in her life. Termination came after a series of stormy exchanges related to this man's pathological control over her life. The relationship began as a well-intentioned effort to nurture and assist someone she loved very much. It ended in severe alienation from her family of origin, depletion of her financial resources, and emotional abuse from her lover.

During that time she remained determined to see only the redeeming qualities in this older man, stubbornly refusing to heed the advice of a circle of friends and family that he was "using" her. She held out against the most objective and reasoned direction this circle of advisers could offer. By the time the relationship collapsed, she was bankrupt: economically, socially, emotionally, morally, and interpersonally. In spite of her valiant efforts to give everything she had to this man, he walked out on her for another woman.

She tearfully shared her experiences, finally admitting to her therapist that she intuitively knew from the very beginning that the arrangement would not work. Now she wished she had listened to this deeper voice of the self and responded to it, rather than working so hard to please the man who had just walked out.

‖ The Notion of Intuition ‖

Webster's dictionary refers to intuition as a perception or view that encompasses an immediate apprehension of truth, or supposed truth, in the absence of conscious rational processes.

In a more poetic expression, Susan L. Taylor identifies intuition with wisdom:

> There is a wisdom that is a part of our being as our flesh and blood and bones: intuition, the deepest knowing....Intuition is a higher form of mind than rational thinking. It's the synthesis of the heart, mind and soul working to expand awareness and understanding. Intuition is the wisdom of the Spirit within us, coaxing us to be fair, to do the right thing, to embrace change as a natural and essential part of life. Intuition is the voice within that is forever pressing us to stretch

ourselves, to take risks, to keep loving and giving birth to a new self. [22]

The intuitive person comes to know truth quickly and unambiguously. It is an illumination, sometimes coming at unexpected moments, which brings with it an unclouded sense of truth about one's self, one's issues, one's future.

Although we believe it touches both sexes equally, women have traditionally expressed greater comfort than men with the experience of intuition but have been reluctant to affirm its value. Current explorations now affirm that women come into maturity by responding openly to the promptings of intuition, and they have stopped apologizing for its efficacy.

"Intuition is the treasure of a woman's psyche," affirms the story-teller Clarissa Pinkola Estes.

It is like a divining instrument and like a crystal through which one can see with uncanny interior vision. It is like a wise old woman who is with you always, *who tells you exactly what the matter is, tells you exactly whether you go left or right.* It is a form of The One Who Knows, old *La Que Sabe,* the Wild Woman. [23]

This renewed trust of intuition invites the women to shift from a self that is based on external authority, to a more real self that comes from within.[24] This inward movement is often described as "listening to our inner voices."

Not only do the women wrestle with questions about trusting their inner voice, so do the men.

A forty-two-year-old priest struggled with persistent anxiety attacks and unexplainable depressed moods during his entire history of service to an eastern diocese.

Medications of various kinds, regular supportive help, and a variety of dysfunctional ways of dealing with his anguish brought no relief. He finally disciplined himself to examine his entire life context in psychotherapy. He disclosed to his therapist that he was the victim of adolescent sexual abuse from a priest-teacher during his years at a prestigious boarding school.

The abusive episodes formed the basis for a series of convoluted, guilt-laden responses that lasted for a lifetime. The abuser ratcheted down his hold on this adolescent by insisting that he showed clear signs of a vocation to the priesthood. After continued prompting and coaching by the abuser, this bright and capable student was accepted for studies for the priesthood. Several years later, he was ordained.

Blessed with a genuine compassion, he functioned well enough to maintain a caring ministry, but his emptiness haunted him mercilessly. The shame, guilt, anxiety and dissociative rituals remained powerful enough to hold him in a structure of life he intuitively never desired. His shame and guilt held him captive for twenty-seven years.

"I never wanted to be a priest in the first place and I spent far too many years living up to someone else's expectations for what I should be." He drew himself upright in his chair, testing again and again the voice that had been mute since early adolescence. "Never again," he repeated, "never again."

This mid-life renaissance became his turning point. From that moment on, he wholeheartedly trusted the directives of his inner voice, explored life through a committed compassion, then altered his complete life structure. His new life now blossoms under the direction of his inner voice.

| The Stages of Developing Trust |

Intuition points more confidently to the summit as it matures and deepens. Its evolution flows with the development of the true self, but contemporary studies approach it from an independent perspective. Belenky, Clinchy, Goldberger and Tarule describe five stages through which women pass in the development of the self, voice, and mind.[25] Although they speak primarily for women, our experience tells us that a similar evolution takes place in the men as they seek a more authentic self.

Stage 1: Silence

This is the stage of disconnectedness from one's own thoughts, voice and power. At this stage, women believe in external authorities only, placing no confidence in their own experiences. We often see this as a stage in which a person holds no real opinions, takes no real risks, and lives in fear of criticism. A defined self is almost non-existent. Life changes at this stage of development leave the person empty, vulnerable, and convinced that it is a fragile and formless proposition. Their lack of a voice allows them to see life as hard and unfeeling.

Stage 2: Received Knowing

In this stage, a woman obtains her identity through conforming to someone else's expectations. She becomes a "good girl," a good student, a good wife. Consequently, another person or an organization maintain control over her life. Many marriages are held together by the power a wife gives to her husband simply because she is fearful of disagreeing with him.

Life is lived in a passive way. Conformity and the need

for approval override all risk-taking. Our experience, how-ever, indicates that men are just as prone to being seduced into conformity by being a "good boy." We find fifty-year-old men who live in terror of displeasing a spouse, a boss, or a religious superior. They spend most of their energy figuring out which way the political wind is blowing, never making a statement of their own unless it echoes the voice of authority.

Stage 3: Subjective Knowing

At this stage, a woman connects with her inner voice for the first time. That could mean a turning away from prevailing opinions, a conflict with external authority, or an arrival at the truth through personal trials. The first encounters with her own truth can be shocking and dra-matic, as she discovers that her perceived self masks a deep disloyalty to her deeper truths.

A personal struggle ensues as she discovers an unbal-ancing dissonance between what others want from her and what she wants for herself. A long period of sifting takes place for her as she tries to weigh her new wisdom. She wrestles with loyalties.

The first halting steps that move toward an authentic self get underway, beginning tentatively, while fears remain strong. She often dreads the loss of long-term rela-tionships, as she reconstructs a new self in opposition to what her friends believe she is.

Stage 4: Procedural Knowing

This stage evolves through difficulty and disillusion-ment, as a woman's knowledge is declared incomplete, unsatisfactory, or inaccurate by some outside authority. Doubts and uncertainties cloud the efforts of her real self to speak. She must work hard to hold on to her truth.

In order to address the challenge with some comfort, she casts about for external reference points. She looks for ways to express the reasons for her beliefs and actions. By doing so, she can lose contact with her inner orientation, again creating doubts about her own truth. Overall, she sifts and assesses, bringing herself back to a sense of trust. The trial by fire is never easy.

Stage 5: Constructed Knowing

This stage marks the integration of inner knowing with the knowledge gained from others. We call it a blending of the inner and outer voices. In the blending is discovered a resolution that is satisfactory for the individual. Even though the sources of the blending are the same for men and women, styles differ significantly. Women tend to be more inclusive in their blending. They are sensitive to the call of compassion. The men seem to have an easier time thinking independently.

Even with the stylistic difference, we suggest that intuition is essentially an inner voice that speaks of one's own truth. It is reliable and trustworthy, but often ignored, suppressed or denied. The pressure to conform, the seduction of compliance, the promise of rewards to come, create such a loud clamor that the inner voice cannot be heard.

‖ Why People Ignore Their Inner Voice ‖

The examples in this chapter suggest an array of reasons why people ignore their inner voices. In the first example, the thirty-year-old woman was involved in an intense, highly romantic love relationship. She was captivated not only by the charm of this ever-elusive male, but she deeply desired to "bring her man to life."

His clinching declaration early in their history that "no one has ever cared about me the way you do; no one has ever offered me such love," became the white noise that dampened down her inner voice. Even though she knew she was being "conned" in a variety of ways, she gave her man the authority to define reality for both of them.

The priest was victimized at an impressionable age by a powerful authority figure. The sexual entanglement, manipulation, and cover-up mechanisms were so overpowering that he was unable to register a voice of protest. Upon admission to the seminary, the rewards of privilege, rank, and mobility in an eastern seaboard high church cocoon, heightened the fantasy of being chosen by God. The public image of a "good boy" buttressed the fantasy until the whole structure collapsed in mid-life.

As seen in these examples, the betrayal of values, integrity, or personal truths cannot be sustained for a lengthy period of time without dysfunctional consequences. Generally, the individual knows they have swapped their integrity for an attractive reward. This knowing brings the stirrings of discomfort usually associated with personal betrayal, but it is laid over with a veneer of firm denial. The price of staying quiet is usually high: the pressings of anxiety or the specter of remorse and guilt. These demons can haunt a person for a lifetime and will only let go when the person aligns his or her inner voice with a more seasoned truth.

Serious reevaluation begins when the person realizes that the tradeoffs have not been worth a life of anguish. The inner voice comes to life and declares, "I should have listened to myself at the time."

Every developmental step proceeds from there on with fear and anxiety. There is often a confession of uncertainty about specific direction, but momentum is maintained by a determination that, "no one is ever going to define my reality for me again." [26]

Learning to Listen to Your Inner Voice

Trusting your deep intuition is the beginning of a different mode of existence. Like the ancient myth of the phoenix bird, new life emerges from the ashes of self-doubt and failure. With these first movements toward the summit of the mountain, latent resources begin to organize around a hunger to deepen the true self. A more clearly defined spirituality begins to come into existence.

The mere desire to soar, however, does not guarantee that deep trust of the self will automatically develop. It needs to be learned, and generally develops over a long period of time. Usually, some work needs to be done to open the way to a deep trust. We suggest several methods below.

Seek and Find Your Solitude

The voice of intuition begins with a whisper. It cannot be heard if the only voices in your life are in the noise of the marketplace or the rattle of inane conversation. Solitude is the essential and quiet context demanded to listen for the voice within. Sam Keen speaks to the men about the importance of solitude in this fashion:

> Solitude begins when a man silences the competing voices of the market, the polis, the home, the mass, and listens to the dictates of his own heart. Self-love requires the same commitment of time and energy as any other relationship. I must take time to be with myself, to discover my desires, my

rhythms, my tastes, my gifts, my hopes, my wounds. We need solitude to keep the relationship between me, myself, and I alive and growing. [27]

In brief, life must quiet down sufficiently to allow you to become sensitized to that quiet voice within you. In solitude, an invitation is extended to the true self to express its desires. Gerald May describes solitude as a call. "Finally," he says, "it calls us onward; it nourishes our spirits and encourages our hearts for whatever may be the next step in our journey towards the Real." [28]

Look at the Patterns in Your Life

It can be shattering to discover that most of your life has been orchestrated by another person, governed solely by the promised rewards of institutional life, or seduced by the unfulfilled promises of love. It can also present the moment of a major reconstruction or turn toward transcendence.

"The moment of truth came to me when I looked at myself in the mirror one morning," he said. "I didn't like what I saw. I hesitated to make eye contact with him. I observed the graying person in the mirror in front of me, and I didn't like him. I didn't trust him. I felt nauseous that this person had never really decided who he is.

"I sat down in a chair, half-shaven and very shaky, and decided I would never accept this person if he did not decide what he really wanted out of life. Then I got angry at myself for allowing so many others to run my life. An hour later, I got out of the chair, talked to the person in the mirror about growing up and getting a life. My emotions surged and I felt a focus, even though I still had goals to set. I started to know myself from that moment, and I have never turned back."

‖ Begin Some Efforts to Develop a Spirituality ‖

Transitions in the inner core of the self take place in a variety of ways, but each one signals the emergence of a more reflective approach to life. Living reflectively is the central process of any adult spirituality. Reflectivity becomes a dialogue between the deepening self and the voices of wisdom that surround us. It is the sifting process applied to every dimension of life.

"What matters in this situation?" the person asks. "What really lasts? What is my inner voice telling me? What do I want to let go of and what do I want to keep? Is God a part of this? If so, how do I learn more about God? What do I need to do to trust this growing voice? How can I be more loyal to my real self?"

Reconstruction begins with the first honest efforts to move toward a resolution. A desire to be whole, to live honestly, or the hunger to develop a true self, usually keep the resolution alive. All forms of spirituality are consolidated in the synthesis of the true self. Intuition becomes the voice flowing from a reflective convergence. Ultimately, it directs the person in all matters.

‖ Intuition and Transitions ‖

As trust deepens, life is lived with peace, confidence, and continuity. Persons know what is appropriate and good for them, even if they cannot clearly define every dimension of their choice. They honestly embrace that which is life-giving and quietly avoid that which is deadening.

Reality becomes unified because the true self is unified. A delightful internal resonance with life all around becomes more real. Some carry the experience of resonance to the level of synchronicity. This is defined by C.G. Jung and others as "meaningful coincidence."[29] This deeply intuitive experience knows that events within one's self and events in the wider universe are intimately connected. They know that nothing really happens by accident. They witness a pleasant convergence of realities as they move confidently in a world that is inviting and friendly. They connect realities in such a way that they live rightly and peacefully.

Some see the physical universe as transparent. It becomes a window through which they enter into a captivating relationship with their personal God.

Is it any wonder, then, that dealing with the reality of change takes on a unique texture during this stage in our process? Some actually know themselves as co-authoring their lives with a loving God.

8.

JOURNALING

Dialogue with the Self

Journaling is nothing more than an exercise of writing a daily record of your thoughts, feelings, and reflections about life. The simple exercise of writing brings an objectivity to obscure thoughts, unnamed feelings, and growing attitudes. Writing gives the developing self a form and substance that is sometimes surprising, but always beneficial. The inner voice moves from a whisper to a self-confident expressiveness. In doing so, a new life story begins to take shape.

Once written, the hidden self is made visible. Sifting becomes more real as options are laid out. A deep appreciation of the feminine spirit evolves. The construction of a better life takes form before your eyes. The dialogue with the inner self is spoken more clearly. Over time, the integration of new wisdom is clearly seen. The handprint of the invisible God becomes visible in one's own script. Many report a deep encounter with the self and an engaging encounter with God as they become comfortable with journaling.

To give you an idea of how the process unfolds, simply imagine yourself journaling your way through some of the experiences we described in the first chapters of this book. Imagine yourself making a sincere effort to express your thoughts and feelings at the time of the event. Read through the following examples and you will understand a little more about what we mean by reflective journaling.

Entry: "Today I sit in the warm sun, feeling its presence on my face and upper body. It renews me. It gives me life. The energy flows into me from the universe, and I become one with it. I'm grateful for the gift of the sunshine."

Entry: "Noontime. I sit in the back of the cathedral church. I feel good about being here. There's a feeling of homecoming, like I felt when I was a child and visited my grandmother. People all around me are praying. I can't pray, but the place captivates me. I'm welcome here. There's a rightness about it. I need to explore what this means for my future. I long to recapture the good feelings about life that I had at one time. Where did they go? I hope I can get them back."

Entry: "That man's eagle dance inspires me. He is so brave to stand in front of that indifferent group and talk openly about his struggles with alcohol and drugs. I feel like I am lifted out of my helplessness. If he can do that with his life, I can surely get myself together."

ǁ Reauthoring a New Life Story ǁ

We will now return to the five processes of change we developed in the main body of this book. We invite you to take each one of these processes, reflect on its relevance for your life at the present time, then use it as a source for journaling. As you follow this simple path, you will discover a great deal about the potential that lies within you. We hope you will enjoy reauthoring the story of your life, trusting your intuition to open up a new future for you.

Process 1: Disintegration

This journaling is to be done when you are confronted with the onset of a major life change. It can evolve at any time, since change never ceases.

Write in your journal precisely what has changed in your life. Is it loss of identity? A collapse of all your values? Sort it out. Is the change on the level of the simple structure of life or does it touch the level of interpersonal loss? Try to describe for yourself what has made this change of such great magnitude. Try to describe the reasons the impact has been so dramatic and so severe. Try, especially, to capture the feelings you are experiencing at this moment.

Write out for yourself some thoughts: What fantasies have now collapsed? When they collapsed, what realization did this collapse bring with it? Has too much of your life been based on fantasy?

Write out for yourself how deep your fantasies run. Do they simply touch the surface structures of your life or do they undergird your entire belief system? Do they influence your view of the transcendent dimension of life? Do they express a deep disappointment in God?

What fantasies are you ready to let go? What real view of life will take their place? Listen quietly for a time to your inner voice. What is it saying about the place in life where you now find yourself? What messages from your inner voice can you now trust? What is unsure for you?

Can you express your experience in terms of soul? Have you lost your soul, or have you begun finding it?

On the third level of loss, what are you feeling? Look back at the signs of grieving from chapter one and see which signs are alive in your experience. Are you anxious? Sad? Angry?

Are you in a stuck position? Is your anger positive or negative? Write out one way that you want your anger to direct your life.

Process 2: Sifting

Your initial task is to sift through the collection of beliefs, attitudes, myths and ideals that have brought you to this place in life. Write:

Which ones are dead? Which ones no longer fit? Which ones do you want to preserve in order to transition through this phase of your life? What ideals still drive you? What beliefs do you want to hang onto? What attitudes about life sustain you?

Do a reflective search of your personal history, complete with its good days and bad days. Write out the story of the worst disappointment you ever experienced. Be as reflective as you possibly can. Assess the deeper foundations of your life. In other words, what brought you through the bad experience; what still motivates you?

Now write out for yourself the story of the most successful experience of your life. Note what has given you the deepest pride and the highest motivation for your life. What brings you the deepest satisfaction?

Spend a few minutes in reflection, then write down the one central value that has governed the course of your life more than any other. Is it love? Is it honesty? Is it greed or double-dealing? Is it compassion? Is it a hard determination not to be beaten? Is it a legacy that was willed to you from your family history? What values have been secondary? How have these other values blended with the central focus for your life?

Now journal the values, attitudes, and direction that you want to retain, and describe how these are going to influence your life from hereon. What you are doing is literally reconstructing a fresh foundation for your life. It will be constructed upon the foundation established through the action of sifting.

Process 3: Reconstructing

This process relates to the practical task of taking the raw materials of an honest and deep reevaluation, then constructing a different approach to life. The hard work of reconstructing begins to consolidate in a new self.

Before asking you to journal, we want to briefly explore the notion of reauthoring a life story. In the story below about a blended family, not just one life story is rewritten, but several. Their shared efforts construct a new experience of family for everyone involved. Perhaps you will see some parallels with your own story as you read it.

‖ Reauthoring Life Stories ‖

"Blending a family has got to be the hardest thing I have ever done," Julie proclaimed. "I have almost parked my dreams that we could ever be a good family. When I was a child, I dreamed of the perfect little family in the suburbs, with everyone so caring and loving toward one another."

The conversation came in the aftermath of another strained and unpleasant week. The blending of the two families, begun only seven months ago, refused to take shape. Constant conflict governed her relationship with Sarah, her husband's teenage daughter.

Julie made several honest efforts to speak about her

concerns to her husband, Phil, but he refused to envision Sarah as Julie described her. Conflict between Phil and Julie then deepened. No matter how much they talked, the gaps between all members of the family refused to close. Sarah's moods then became a powerful factor in the emotional life of the family. Over a period of months, she learned to use them to control everyone's comfort, spontaneity, and their capacity to interact freely.

Julie's tears stopped for awhile as she assessed the situation. It became clear to her therapist that she evaluated the health of the family on the basis of the continued shake-up caused by Sarah's moods. Her therapist then invited her to examine a few other dimensions of her life before drawing any final conclusions about success or failure.

At first, Julie could see few genuine successes, but after some prompting, she began to refocus. It became clear that everyone in the family got along quite well, except Sarah. Julie and Phil enjoyed life together. When they broke away for brief vacations, they found their closeness revitalizing. They joined their economic resources together and now lived in a large and comfortable suburban home. They still found their friendship maturing. In brief, Julie began to understand that Sarah's moods clouded her capacity to see any other success in the family. This, in turn, gave Sarah far too much power over Julie's life.

Once Julie reexamined her life from a larger perspective, she realized that she had allowed Sarah to consume too much of her time and energy. That simple insight helped her accomplish the therapist's second suggestion: to place less emphasis on Sarah's moods.

It took a great deal of effort at first, but the alliances and distribution of energy in the family began to shift. This shift allowed Julie to finally understand that she equated success or failure with Sarah's emotional reactivity. In effect, control of the family belonged to Sarah, not to Phil and Julie.

Julie's therapist then assisted her to honestly underscore her real successes, feel positive about her genuine strengths, and no longer hand over raw power to a moody teenager. A major shift in the balance of power in the family came when Phil and Julie determined to host a family conference on a weekly basis. The conferences would include all five children, with no exceptions. As these conferences developed, every family member learned lessons about the importance of working in a cooperative fashion.

The results of the restructuring were significant. The family nullified the power of Sarah's moods by simply working around them. This pushed Sarah to find more appropriate ways to deal with her ups and downs. The improved atmosphere in the family then allowed Julie to let go of some of her resentments. She responded positively to her husband's support, and they grew closer.

Once removed from her position of power in the family, Sarah decided to become easier to live with. Every family member felt better about that. As the peaceful atmosphere in the family became more real, a few of Julie's old dreams returned. She discovered that in even the most perfect family, there are problems to be worked out. Family members learned to share positive feelings, and this helped them become more sensitive to one another's differences.

Over time, each family member cooperated in re-authoring their personal stories. They still contribute equally to rewriting the story of the family. Difficulties remain at times, but their optimism sustains them.

Take your journal again and write: What parallels do you see in this story and what is going on in your life?

Write out three shifts in the ways that you now look at your reality, compared to this time last month. If the shifts are not apparent, what has changed in the last year?

No doubt the shifts represent changes in values, differences in attitudes, or new perspectives that evolve out of a critical self-examination.

Think of each of these changes as a small building block for success. Write in your journal how the building blocks you describe will enable you to reconstruct. What form will the reconstruction take? In what practical ways do you plan to reconstruct? Are you intending to reconstruct only your life story, or will you invite someone else to join you?

Write again in your journal: describe the internal component in your reconstruction process. In what ways is your developing self reflecting the external changes in your life? Can you rely on this developing self to offer you continuity from day to day?

Now sit quietly again and read the results of your writing. What is your inner voice saying to you? Can you trust it any more now than before you began writing?

Process 4: Reintegrating

The newness of life now begins to blossom in a renewed and confident self. Like an internal guidance system, the true self begins to take on a more active role. The self begins to open up a higher consciousness while at the same time seeking a compassionate connection with the world.

Take out your journal and write down your dreams. Let your imagination take you to the heights. Write out everything you have ever desired to achieve and build. Read your dreams out loud.

Write down which dreams have been fulfilled and which ones are still lacking. Also write out which dreams cause you the deepest regret and which ones continue to fill you with energy.

Write down one simple decision about which dreams you want to pursue and those which you wish to drop. Write out what your inner voice is telling you about which to drop and which to claim. Trust it!

Now write a story of your life from the perspective of ten years from this day. Where will you be? How will you spend your energy? What are you willing to live or die for?

Now read your story aloud to yourself and let it speak to you about a number of realities:

What values still govern your story?
What dreams are still alive?
In what ways have your dreams matured?
Do you still hold on to childhood fantasies that are problematic?
What obstacles (either within you or in your world) need to be moved out of the way in order for your dreams to be fulfilled?

Process 5: Transcendence: Oklahoma City Revisited

Life is lived, decisions are made, directions sought through the promptings of the voice of intuition.

It is months later. The leering icon of the bombed-out federal building is gone. In its place is a vacant lot, laid over with heavy gravel. The open space is surrounded by a high fence. Pilgrims approach the fence reverently. It becomes a wailing wall. For some, it is a memorial, like the Vietnam Veterans' Memorial wall in the nation's capital.

The pilgrims leave their gifts at the foot of the fence or fasten them to its heavy chain links. The fence now supports a collection of flowers, T-shirts decorated with messages of hope, American flags, religious symbols, teddy bears, and random memorabilia from the hearts of those who remember that day of death. Messages to the dead and the living are typed or scribbled on looseleaf papers of all kinds, then left behind for others to read.

Two miles away at the state capitol complex, the pilgrims plant a cluster of new trees. Each tree is dedicated to someone who lost a life in the explosion. The young trees mark the beginning of a memorial garden, to be completed as the collection of ideas consolidate into a cohesive plan.

The sun begins to set. A small group holds hands in a circle, surrounding a freshly planted tree. The group prays aloud for all the victims and their families. Other visitors, scattered here and there around the capitol grounds, pray for the human race. Others weep quietly.

Make an entry in your journal. Assume that your entry will be posted on the chain-link fence surrounding the federal building site. Assume your note will be read by the hundreds who pass by each day, looking for some sign of life in this sacred space.

When you have finished your note, read it and listen to what your inner voice is telling you.

Notes

1. William Bridges, *Managing Transitions: Making the Most of Change* (Reading, PA, Addison-Wesley, 1991), pp. 24-25.

2. Julia Cameron, *The Artist's Way: A Spiritual Path to Higher Creativity* (New York: Putnam, 1992), p. 60.

3. Kathleen Norris, *Dakota: A Spiritual Geography* (New York: Ticknor and Fields, 1993), p. 83.

4. Susan L. Taylor, *In the Spirit* (New York: Amistad, 1993), p. 83.

5. Christina Feldman and Jack Kornfield, *Stories of the Spirit, Stories of the Heart: Parables of the Spiritual Path From Around the World* (San Francisco: Harper, 1991), p. 143.

6. Phil Cousineau, "Soulfullness Is a Verb." Richard Carlson and Benjamin Shield, eds., *Handbook for the Soul* (Boston: Little, Brown and Company, 1995), p. 161.

7. Lynn Andrews, "Earth, Body and Spirit." Richard Carlson and Benjamin Shield, eds., *Handbook for the Soul*, pp. 95-96.

8. Dhyani Ywahoo, *Voices of Our Ancestors* (Boston: Shambala, 1987), p. 161.

9. Joseph Goldstein and Jack Kornfield, *Seeking the Heart of Wisdom* (Boston: Shambala, 1987), p. 66.

10. James F. Masterson, M.D., *The Search for the Real Self* (New York: The Free Press, 1988), p. 23.

11. Susan L. Taylor, *Lessons in Living* (New York: Doubleday, 1995), p. 42.

12. James F. Masterson, M.D., *The Search for the Real Self*, p. 50.

13. Jacquelin Small, *Transformers* (Marina Del Rey, CA: DeVorss and Co., 1982), p. 242.

14. Sam Keen, *Hymns to an Unknown God* (New York: Bantam, 1994), p. 148.

15. Robert L. Keck, *Sacred Eyes* (Indianapolis, IN: Knowledge Systems, Inc., 1992), p. 230.

16. Gerald May, M.D., *Will and Spirit* (San Francisco: Harper, 1982), p. 64.

17. Cameron, *The Artist's Way*, p. 14.

18. Anne C. Carr, *A Search for Wisdom and Spirit* (Notre Dame, IN: University of Notre Dame Press, 1988), p. 3.

19. Thomas Merton, *New Seeds of Contemplation* (New York: New Directions, 1961), p. 36.

20. Ibid., p. 7.

21. Ibid., p. 36.

22. Taylor, *In the Spirit*, p. 55.

23. Clarissa Pinkola Estes, Ph.D., *Women Who Run With the Wolves* (New York: Ballantine Books, 1992), p. 74.

24. Carol Gilligan, *In a Different Voice* (Cambridge: Harvard University Press, 1982), p. 2.

25. Mary Field Belenky, Blythe McVicker Clinchy, Nancy Rule Goldberger, and Jill Mattuck Tarule, *Women's Ways of Knowing* (New York: Basic Books, 1986), p. 24 ff.

26. Ibid., p. 77.

27. Sam Keen, *Fire in the Belly*, (New York: Bantam Books, 1991), p. 161.

28. May, *Will and Spirit*, p. 316.

29. Jean Shinoda Bolin, M.D., *The Tao of Psychology: Synchronicity and the Self* (San Francisco: Harper, 1979), p. 16 ff.

Other Books by Patrick J. and Clauette M.
McDonald
Published by Paulist Press

The Soul of a Marriage

Soul Work: A Workbook for Couples

Can Your Marriage Be a Friendship?